"Are there ways of improving engagement with psychological treatment like CBT? Any counsellor, therapist, manager or policy-maker interested in this question will find this book a breath of fresh air. It breaks down the barriers between treatment approaches to consider how motivational interviewing might be integrated with CBT. The useful practical details are here, along with an openness to innovation that will serve our clients well. As such, this book is ground-breaking."

—Stephen Rollnick, Professor of Clinical Psychology
at Cardiff University and co-founder of
Motivational Interviewing

T0299790

Motivational Cognitive Behavioural Therapy

This informative and straightforward book explores the emergence of motivational interviewing (MI) and cognitive behavioural therapy (CBT), with specific attention given to the increasing focus on the central importance of the therapeutic alliance in improving client outcomes.

Comprising 30 short chapters divided into two parts – theory and practice – this entry in the popular *CBT Distinctive Features* series covers the key features of MI-informed CBT, offering essential guidance for students and practitioners experienced in both MI and CBT, as well as practitioners from other theoretical orientations who require an accessible guide to this developing approach.

Cathy Atkinson is Curriculum Director of the Doctorate in Educational and Child Psychology programme, and a Senior Lecturer at the University of Manchester, UK. She is also a registered practitioner educational psychologist, specialising in therapeutic approaches for students accessing alternative provision for social, emotional and mental health difficulties, and co-founder of the Manchester Motivational Interviewing Network, which seeks to promote and support multiagency MI practice across the north-west of England.

Paul Earnshaw is a Senior Psychological Therapist working for Greater Manchester Mental Health NHS Foundation Trust, UK. He is an active member of the Motivational Interviewing Network of Trainers (MINT) and has developed and contributed to workshops and symposiums in that forum. His long-standing interest and practice have been on the integration of CBT and MI. He is also a co-founder of the Manchester Motivational Interviewing Network.

CBT Distinctive Features

Series Editor: Windy Dryden

Cognitive behaviour therapy (CBT) occupies a central position in the move towards evidence-based practice and is frequently used in the clinical environment. Yet there is no one universal approach to CBT and clinicians speak of first-, second-, and even third-wave approaches.

This series provides straightforward, accessible guides to a number of CBT methods, clarifying the distinctive features of each approach. The series editor, Windy Dryden, successfully brings together experts from each discipline to summarise the 30 main aspects of their approach divided into theoretical and practical features.

The *CBT Distinctive Features* series will be essential reading for psychotherapists, counsellors and psychologists of all orientations who want to learn more about the range of new and developing cognitive behaviour approaches.

Recent titles in the series:

Cognitive Behavioural Chairwork by Matthew Pugh

Emotional Schema Therapy by Robert L. Leahy

Mindfulness-Based Cognitive Therapy, 2nd edition, by Rebecca Crane

For further information about this series please visit
www.routledge.com/CBT-Distinctive-Features/book-series/DFS

Motivational Cognitive Behavioural Therapy

Distinctive Features

Cathy Atkinson and Paul Earnshaw

Routledge
Taylor & Francis Group

LONDON AND NEW YORK

First published 2020
by Routledge
2 Park Square, Milton Park, Abingdon, Oxon OX14 4RN

and by Routledge
52 Vanderbilt Avenue, New York, NY 10017

Routledge is an imprint of the Taylor & Francis Group, an informa business

British Library Cataloguing-in-Publication Data
A catalogue record for this book is available from the British Library

Library of Congress Cataloging-in-Publication Data
A catalog record has been requested for this book

ISBN: 978-0-367-07457-9 (hbk)
ISBN: 978-0-367-07458-6 (pbk)
ISBN: 978-0-429-02089-6 (ebk)

Typeset in Times New Roman
by codeMantra

Contents

Figures and tables

Figures

Tables

Acknowledgements

CA – It is almost 20 years since I started researching motivational interviewing (MI) within the context of educational psychology practice and to be writing this now feels like the culmination of a journey, yet to be finished. Thank you to all of the people who have helped me along this journey. To Eddie McNamara, who brought MI to the educational psychology profession almost at its advent and who has been a continual source of support, encouragement and enthusiasm. To Professor Kevin Woods, who supervised my original MI Master's assignment which set me on this path, who co-authored my first MI paper with me and has co-authored subsequent papers, always challenging and shaping my thinking. To educational psychology students Sarah Cryer, Louise Jones, Michelle Kittles, Laura Snape and Jill Simpson who have studied MI tirelessly as part of their doctoral research and helped contribute to the evidence base around school-based MI.

Thank you to members of the Manchester Motivational Interviewing Network (MMIN) who have brought new opportunities for knowledge enhancement and practice development, particularly Sarah Parry and Lis Cordingley; and to Joanna Bragg and George Thomas for all the research support and development. I could not have asked for more from my colleagues. Without the MMIN, I would never have met Paul, my co-author, from whom I have learned so much about both MI and CBT and with whom it has been an absolute pleasure to collaborate with on this book.

Thank you to my parents, Philip and Bette, and to my brothers, Dave and Rob, for all the help and support over the years. To Steve. I know I always try to cram in too much anyway and that maybe writing a book as well was probably a step too far. Let's find more time for riding bikes together once it's done. Finally, to Anneliese and Spencer. I know that the dearth of wizards and witches will mean that at this moment in time the book will not be of much interest – you've told me so yourselves! However, I hope that at some point in the future, MI will offer you some of the things that it has offered me, in terms of giving me a framework for at least trying to be empathic, accepting and compassionate in my interactions with others; and in understanding why these things are important.

PE – To all of the clients that I have worked with over the years who have taught me how to have motivational conversations. As a psychological therapist and CBT practitioner for 17 years, they have shown me how MI can be integrated with CBT, for both the benefit of the clients and the therapists that work alongside them.

Also thanks to Professors Christine Barrowclough and Gillian Haddock leading figures in BABCP (British Association for Behavioural and Cognitive Psychotherapies). They had the foresight to develop and evaluate an integration of motivational interviewing and cognitive behaviour therapy for psychosis (MICBT) in a large randomised controlled trial.

Working in this study from 2004, I developed my interest in what these therapies can and do offer each other. Through this work, I met my colleague Rory Allott, and we have collaborated in the development of training in the integration of motivational interviewing with CBT, across the globe.

Many thanks to all those colleagues within the motivational interviewing network of trainers (MINT) for their generous contributions in discussions and training events. They have encouraged me to develop my knowledge and expertise in this field.

My co-author Cathy Atkinson and I met through our mutual interest in theory, research and practice in MI. It has been a pleasure and an inspiration to work with Cathy both on this book and as part of the MMIN.

Finally, I dedicate this work to my partner Steph and our brilliant children Ella and Theo, who are always there for me.

Permission acknowledgements

Grateful acknowledgement is made to the following for permission to reprint previously published material:

Figure 6.1 was provided by Professor Richard Ryan and Shannon Ceresoli, Director of the Center for Self-Determination Theory (CSDT).

Figure 7.1 is adapted from McNamara, E. (2009). *Motivational Interviewing: Theory, Practice and Applications with Children and Young People*. Ainsdale: Positive Behaviour Management.

Figure 7.2 is reproduced from Booth Butterfield, S. (2017). Communication for a change. Retrieved May 28, 2019, from http://healthyinfluence.com/wordpress/steves-primer-of-practical-persuasion-3-0/intro/stages-of-change/ and is based on the work of Professor James Prochaska and colleagues.

Figure 11.1 is adapted from Copeland, L., McNamara, R., Kelson, M., & Simpson, S. (2015). Mechanisms of change within motivational interviewing in relation to health behaviors outcomes: A systematic review. *Patient Education and Counseling, 98*(4), 401–411. doi:10.1016/j.pec.2014.11.022

Thank you to Professor William Miller for permission to reproduce Figures 8.1, 8.2 and 17.1 which originally appeared in Miller, W. R., & Rollnick, S. (2013). *Motivational Interviewing, Third Edition: Helping People Change*. New York: Guilford Press, and to use the card sort activity hyperlink, referred to in Chapter 25.

Abbreviations

ACT	Acceptance and commitment therapy
CBT	Cognitive behavioural therapy
CBT(p)	Cognitive behavioural therapy for psychosis
CEMI	Client evaluation of motivational interviewing
CFT	Compassion focussed therapy
CTS-R	Revised cognitive training scales
DBT	Dialectical behaviour therapy
EPE	Elicit-provide-elicit
FRAMES	Feedback, responsibility, advice, menu of options, empathy, self-efficacy
GAS	Goal attainment scaling
MBCBT	Mindfulness-based cognitive behaviour therapy
MCT	Meta cognitive therapy
MI	Motivational interviewing
MICBT	Motivational interviewing and cognitive behavioural therapy
MICTS	Motivational interviewing cognitive training scales
MIFI	Motivational interviewing focusing instrument
MITI	Motivational interviewing treatment integrity (scale)

OARS	Open-ended questions, affirmations, reflections and summaries
OCD	Obsessive-compulsive disorder
SDT	Self-determination theory
TTM	Transtheoretical model

Introduction

There is a large and developing evidence base indicating the success of CBT across multiple domains. However, one issue which is often overlooked in CBT literature and practice is consideration of client motivation for engagement and persistence with therapy. Marker and Norton (2018) reported figures suggesting almost a quarter of clients receiving CBT for anxiety drop out, with 15%–50% not responding to treatment. Even in the face of all of the positive findings for CBT's effectiveness, these figures make salutary reading and suggest room for improvement. This book considers theory and practice issues relating to motivation within CBT. Specifically it does this by considering how motivational interviewing (MI) theory and practice can be integrated within CBT and indeed with other therapeutic approaches.

CBT works on the premise that cognitive activity affects behaviours; that this can be monitored and altered; and that desired behaviour change can be effected through cognitive change (Dobson, 2007, p. 4). Within these propositions, an important word is "desired". When clients meet with therapists in a state of readiness to overcome a behaviour that has become problematic for them, it is assumed there is motivation to work on the behaviour. But what happens to clients who are not sure if they really want to change? Who are frightened or intimidated by the thought of change? Who believe themselves to be incapable of change?

MI developed initially in the fields of addiction and substance use (Miller, 1983) as a way of working with clients, often who had been referred by a third party and had not necessarily reached a point at which they perceived their behaviour to be problematic or wanted to change. Atkinson and Woods (2003) noted that MI is based on the idea that clients do not necessarily enter into therapeutic consultations in a state of readiness to change patterns of, for example, substance use, exercise or diet, and that the aim of the therapy may be about achieving some sort of "social control" (p. 51); or perhaps a medical prognosis preferable to the doctor or clinician. Furthermore, it acknowledges that there may be strong factors influencing clients' decision to continue to engage in behaviours which may be seen as problematic by others.

MI is a collaborative style of conversation aimed at resolving ambivalence and strengthening commitment to change (Miller & Rollnick, 2013). It is an approach which we believe, and which an emerging body of research is starting to suggest, can enrich what CBT can offer, particularly for clients who might find it difficult to engage, or persist with therapy. Furthermore, the detailed description of what are often referred to as 'general' or non-specific' factors, essentially the skills involved in developing and maintaining the therapeutic alliance, allowing the client a safe space to explore, evaluate and challenge their own patterns of behaviour, may be offered more clearly through MI than CBT (cf. Driessen & Hollon, 2011). Thus within this book we argue that the relational skills specified within MI can complement the sophisticated and well-defined technical skills which CBT utilises in promoting positive outcomes for clients.

In their systematic literature review and meta-analysis, Marker and Norton (2018) found that providing MI as an adjunct to CBT improved post-treatment outcomes for anxiety disorders. However, the authors suggested that treatment drop-out could be reduced by a more integrated approach, which did not require a clear demarcation between CBT and MI.

While it is acknowledged that the evidence for the effectiveness of an integrated approach needs to be established (Marker & Norton, 2018), this book aims to offer templates for how CBT and MI theory and practice can be integrated to form a flexible, context-responsive and client-centred approach which can maximise engagement and outcomes. Whether as a prelude to

CBT, as a combined approach, or as an integrative framework, we believe that MI has a lot to offer to CBT theory and practice, and vice versa.

The term we will use to describe this approach within this book is MICBT (motivational interviewing and cognitive behavioural therapy). We acknowledge that MICBT may take many guises, which could relate to various different issues: the background, training and experience of the therapist; the therapeutic context; and perhaps most importantly, the needs and aspirations of the client. From this perspective, integration can be flexible, emergent or practised from a needs-led basis. We are not seeking to prescribe how therapists should undertake MICBT, but instead to provide theoretical and practical structures for integrated practice.

The first 15 chapters of this book explore the distinct theoretical features of MICBT. We start by introducing the history and background of MI, before considering its theoretical emergence and how this is relevant to CBT practice. We consider core elements of the MI philosophy, including the spirit (Miller & Rollnick, 2013) and principles (Miller & Rollnick, 2002), before highlighting some of the evidence for both the effectiveness of MICBT and for why particular MI components might enhance practice. We finish the first part of the book by considering similarities and differences between CBT and MI, and between MI and other CBT-based approaches.

In the second section of the book, we seek to offer practical and tangible guidance to therapists who wish to incorporate aspects of MI into their practice. We outline the central MI processes of engaging, focusing, evoking and planning, before illustrating the four core skills of open questions, affirmations, reflections and summaries. We then move on to offering frameworks for structuring sessions, exploring values and providing information, before finishing by exploring wider practice issues – training, fidelity, working at a systemic level and ethics.

Throughout the book, the terms 'therapist' and 'client' will be used consistently to describe the facilitator of, and customer for MICBT. We acknowledge that these terms may not resonate with readers working in certain settings, for example in education or healthcare, where the roles might be defined differently, and hope this will not provide a distraction.

We have learned a lot from writing this book together. Our conversations have helped clarify ambiguities within our own theoretical knowledge and offered us both new strategies and ideas for practice. We very much hope that you will find the book useful in exploring your own knowledge and experience of therapeutic practice, and in finding new ways to offer the very best support to the clients you work with.

References

Atkinson, C., & Woods, K. (2003). Motivational interviewing strategies for disaffected secondary school students: A case example. *Educational Psychology in Practice, 19*(1), 49–64.

Dobson, K. S. (Ed). (2007). *Handbook of cognitive-behavioral therapies*: Third edition. London: Guilford Press.

Driessen, E., & Hollon, S. D. (2011). Motivational interviewing from a cognitive behavioral perspective. *Cognitive and Behavioral Practice, 18*(1), 70–73. doi:10.1016/j.cbpra.2010.02.007

Marker, I., & Norton, P. J. (2018). The efficacy of incorporating motivational interviewing to cognitive behavior therapy for anxiety disorders: A review and meta-analysis. *Clinical Psychology Review, 62*(April), 1–10. doi:10.1016/j.cpr.2018.04.004

Miller, W. R. (1983). Motivational interviewing with problem drinkers. *Behavioural Psychotherapy, 11*(2), 147–172. doi:10.1017/S0141347300006583

Miller, W. R., & Rollnick, S. (2002). *Motivational interviewing, second edition: Preparing people for change*. New York: Guilford Press.

Miller, W. R., & Rollnick, S. (2013). *Motivational interviewing, third edition: Helping people change*. New York: Guilford Press.

Part I

THE DISTINCTIVE THEORETICAL FEATURES OF MICBT

1

The history of motivational interviewing

The first chapter will introduce readers to motivational interviewing (MI). It will chart its emergence via William Miller's initial articulation of the approach to Norwegian psychology students, through to its development within practice in substance use, healthcare, and a whole range of other contexts. It will highlight the rationale for the focus on resolving ambivalence within therapy. Further it will describe the potential contribution of MI to CBT practice, which will be the main theme of this book.

Background

Miller and Rose (2009) recalled the early work of William Miller who, as Professor of Psychiatry and Psychology at the University of New Mexico (Miller, 2019) in the early 1980s, explored the impact of interpersonal skills on the effectiveness of behavioural therapy for clients who were problem drinkers. Subsequently Miller completed a sabbatical at the Hjellestad Clinic and University of Bergen, Norway, during which his description of his clinical practice to resident psychologists led him to devise the first conceptual model of MI, which was subsequently published (Miller, 1983).

Later, on a sabbatical in Sydney, Australia, Miller met Stephen Rollnick, a South African psychologist working in the UK who was already using MI within clinical practice. This led to production of the seminal text *Motivational Interviewing: Preparing People to Change Addictive Behaviour* (Miller & Rollnick, 1991). Atkinson and Woods (2017) described how subsequent volumes (Miller & Rollnick, 2002, 2013) further developed the approach, sometimes with quite significant changes to its central structure and theoretical position. Throughout its journey, the concepts of exploring ambivalence and strengthening commitment to behavioural change have remained central to MI (Atkinson & Woods, 2017).

Developments

Early conceptualisation (Miller & Rollnick, 1991) linked MI closely with the transtheoretical model (TTM) (Prochaska & DiClemente, 1982) (see Chapter 6), which proposed that clients pass through a series of stages – from precontemplation, or not really even considering change, through to maintenance and keeping the change going. Later, these ideas become less central (Miller & Rollnick, 2002), although for some practitioners, they had become synonymous (Atkinson & Amesu, 2007). Miller and Rollnick (2009) clarified the distinction between MI and the TTM and proposed that the MI spirit (see Chapter 8) should define practice. Later publications (Miller & Rollnick, 2002, 2013) have emphasised the relational and communicative aspects of MI, introducing processes and skills which are fundamental to developing a strong therapeutic alliance.

MI has become an extremely popular approach. It is widely used within healthcare and drug and alcohol services, but its application now branches to numerous and diverse fields and across international contexts, supported by its strong empirical foundations and the extensive work of researchers across different fields (Miller & Moyers, 2017).

The central role of ambivalence in MI

Miller and Moyers (2017) described how MI addresses the frustrating issue of reluctance to change despite advice to do so. While many therapeutic modalities, including CBT, assume readiness for change, MI acknowledges that clients are often ambivalent about change. Miller and Rollnick (2013) proposed that "ambivalence is simultaneously wanting and not wanting something or wanting both of two incompatible things" (p. 6). For example, a smoker might enjoy the social and relaxation benefits of cigarettes while being concerned about the health and financial costs. MI was designed specifically to strengthen clients' motivation for change (Miller & Moyers, 2017).

How can MI support CBT?

While CBT should assess motivation (Roth & Pilling, 2007), it places far less emphasis on developing client motivation for change. As such, MI has been seen as both a useful precursor to CBT (Kertes, Westra, Angus, & Marcus, 2011; Marker & Norton, 2018) and a method that can be integrated to engage clients who may not readily engage with CBT approaches (Driessen & Hollon, 2011).

Miller and Rollnick (2009) proposed that cognitive behavioural approaches "generally involve providing clients with something they are assumed to lack" (p. 134) such as psychoeducation or new coping skills. MI instead assumes that the skills and solutions lie with the client and the therapeutic partnership involves working together to find them. We are not suggesting that one of these approaches is wrong and the other is right. Instead, within this book, we hope to illustrate the strengths of both approaches and describe how they can be potentially combined to maximise outcomes for clients.

Summary

1. MI was developed to support problem drinkers, but it has since emerged as a leading therapeutic approach, with a strong evidence base across multiple contexts.

2. At the heart of MI is the concept of ambivalence, or feeling two ways about something. MI seeks specifically to build motivation for change.
3. MI can be combined with CBT to maximise outcomes for clients.

References

Atkinson, C., & Amesu, M. (2007). Using solution-focused approaches in motivational interviewing with young people. *Pastoral Care in Education*, *25*, 31–37. doi:10.1111/j.1468-0122.2007.00405.x

Atkinson, C., & Woods, K. (2017). Establishing theoretical stability and treatment integrity for motivational interviewing. *Behavioural and Cognitive Psychotherapy*, *45*(4), 337–350. doi:10.1017/S1352465817000145

Driessen, E., & Hollon, S. D. (2011). Motivational interviewing from a cognitive behavioral perspective. *Cognitive and Behavioral Practice*, *18*(1), 70–73. doi:10.1016/j.cbpra.2010.02.007

Kertes, A., Westra, H. A., Angus, L., & Marcus, M. (2011). The impact of motivational interviewing on client experiences of cognitive behavioral therapy for generalized anxiety disorder. *Cognitive and Behavioral Practice*, *18*(1), 55–69. doi:10.1016/j.cbpra.2009.06.005

Marker, I., & Norton, P. J. (2018). The efficacy of incorporating motivational interviewing to cognitive behavior therapy for anxiety disorders: A review and meta-analysis. *Clinical Psychology Review*, *62*(April), 1–10. doi:10.1016/j.cpr.2018.04.004

Miller, W. R. (1983). Motivational interviewing with problem drinkers. *Behavioural Psychotherapy*, *11*(2), 147–172. doi:10.1017/S0141347300006583

Miller, W. R. (2019). William R. Miller. Retrieved December 31, 2018, from http://www.williamrmiller.net/index.html

Miller, W. R., & Moyers, T. B. (2017). Motivational interviewing and the clinical science of Carl Rogers. *Journal of Consulting and Clinical Psychology*, *85*(8), 757–766. doi:10.1037/ccp0000179

Miller, W. R., & Rollnick, S. (1991). *Motivational interviewing: Preparing people to change addictive behaviour*. New York: Guilford Press.

Miller, W. R., & Rollnick, S. (2002). *Motivational interviewing: Preparing people for change*. 2nd edition. New York: Guilford Press.

Miller, W. R., & Rollnick, S. (2009). Ten things that motivational interviewing is not. *Behavioural and Cognitive Psychotherapy, 37,* 129–140. doi:10.1017/S1352465809005128

Miller, W. R., & Rollnick, S. (2013). *Motivational interviewing, third edition: Helping People Change.* New York: Guilford Press.

Miller, W. R., & Rose, G. S. (2009). Toward a theory of motivational interviewing. *The American Psychologist, 64*(6), 527–537. doi:10.1037/a0016830

Prochaska, J. O., & DiClemente, C. C. (1982). Transtheoretical therapy: Toward a more integrative model of change. *Psychotherapy: Theory Research and Practice, 19*(3), 276–288.

Roth, A. D., & Pilling, S. (2007). *The competences required to deliver effective cognitive and behavioural therapy for people with depression and with anxiety disorders.* London: Department of Health.

2

Defining MICBT

This chapter will set out the core definitions of MI, CBT and MICBT, before looking at how these potentially direct theory and practice.

Definitions of MI

Definitions of MI have evolved over the years (Miller & Rollnick, 1991, 2002, 2013). Most recently (Miller & Rollnick, 2013, p. 29) offered three separate definitions of MI.

> **Layperson's definition:** "Motivational interviewing is a collaborative conversation style for strengthening a person's own motivation and commitment to change".
>
> **Practitioner's definition:** "Motivational Interviewing is a person-centred counselling style for addressing the common problem of ambivalence about change".
>
> **Technical definition:** "Motivational interviewing is a collaborative, goal-orientated style of communication with particular attention to the language of change. It is designed to strengthen personal motivation for and commitment to a specific goal by eliciting and exploring the person's own reasons for change within an atmosphere or acceptance and compassion."

Central to all three is the notion of ambivalence, or feeling two ways about something – such as acknowledging the health benefits which might result from losing weight, but not particularly wanting to engage in a diet or exercise regime that might bring about such changes. In their early paper "What is Motivational Interviewing?" Rollnick and Miller (1995) proposed that MI was more focused and goal-directed than non-directive counselling, with the resolution of ambivalence being its central purpose.

Miller and Rollnick (2013) used the metaphor of having an "internal committee inside your mind" (p. 7) to describe ambivalence. Within this "committee" the client hears arguments for and against change. If they are then presented with arguments for change from the therapist, these are only siding with one set of perspectives held by the "committee", so a natural response is for the client then to provide arguments or reasons for not changing. This can make the client appear defensive or resistant. The therapist trying to help the client by arguing for changes which they believe to be beneficial or in the client's best interest can be linked to what is known as the "righting reflex" (see Chapter 16).

Definitions of CBT

Beck (1979) proposed that CBT was based on the underlying theoretical principle that an individual's emotions and thought processes are largely determined by the way in which they understand and structure the world. Techniques can then be used to help explore and test particular misconceptions and maladaptive assumptions and strategies. Roth and Pilling (2007) identified three important features of CBT:

1. That CBT is intended to be collaborative and that the client should be encouraged to share responsibility for working through the therapy.
2. Therapists should maintain a sense that CBT should promote clients' ability to understand themselves through guided discovery.
3. CBT should help clients learn skills to help them deal with future situations more effectively.

These features are particularly important to consider within the context of an MI-informed intervention, as all relate to promoting the client's autonomy, self-efficacy and responsibility for change. In fact, Randall and McNeil (2017, p. 309) state that "MI and CBT are like half-siblings who share one parent. Their partially shared theoretical backgrounds make the two approaches well suited to be paired."

Definition of MICBT

To date, to the best of the authors' knowledge, a specific definition of MICBT has not been proposed. Miller (2017) describes how MI was initially designed as a precursor to therapy and was later redefined as a more holistic approach following positive research findings. Naar and Safren (2017) offer three ways in which MI can be used in conjunction with CBT.

1. As a pre-session intervention to build motivation for change
2. At points during a CBT intervention when ambivalence arises, or when motivational factors present a potential barrier
3. As a fully integrated approach.

In relation to the third approach, the authors would argue that this might include a CBT intervention within which the spirit, processes and skills of MI contribute to the ethos and structure of the overall therapeutic approach. On the basis of these descriptions, the authors would like to propose the following definition of MICBT:

> MICBT is a therapeutic approach to supporting clients who may be ambivalent about change through using components of MI and CBT in a sequential, interchangeable, partially or fully integrated manner.

Randall and McNeil (2017) suggested that integrating MI and CBT is "ripe with possibilities" (p. 308) for improving practice and promoting client outcomes. It is hoped that this book will address possibilities for practitioners to look at opportunities for meaningful integration within their professional contexts.

Summary

1. The notion of understanding the client's ambivalence about change is central to definitions of MI.
2. Both MI and CBT recognise the importance of the client taking responsibility for change and use approaches which support this.
3. There are different ways in which MI can be used with CBT, from using MI as a precursor to CBT, to using the approaches in a fully integrated way. Future chapters will explore possibilities for practitioners.

References

Beck, A. T. (1979). *Cognitive therapy of depression*. New York: Guilford Press.

Miller, W. R. (2017). *Taking the lower place: Motivational interviewing and social dominance*. Malahide, Ireland, October 5: 20th anniversary Forum of the Motivational Interviewing Network of Trainers.

Miller, W. R., & Rollnick, S. (1991). *Motivational interviewing: Preparing people to change addictive behaviour*. New York: Guilford Press.

Miller, W. R., & Rollnick, S. (2002). *Motivational interviewing, second edition: Preparing people for change*. New York: Guilford Press.

Miller, W. R., & Rollnick, S. (2013). *Motivational interviewing, third edition: Helping people change*. New York: Guilford Press.

Naar, S., & Safren, S. A. (2017). *Motivational interviewing and CBT: Combining strategies for maximum effectiveness*. New York: Guilford Press.

Randall, C. L., & McNeil, D. W. (2017). Motivational interviewing as an adjunct to cognitive behavior therapy for anxiety disorders: a critical review of the literature. *Cognitive and Behavioral Practice*, *24*(3), 296–311. doi:10.1016/j.cbpra.2016.05.003

Rollnick, S., & Miller, W. R. (1995). What is motivational interviewing? *Behavioural and Cognitive Psychotherapy*, *23*, 325–334. doi:10.1017/S135246580001643X

Roth, A. D., & Pilling, S. (2007). *The competences required to deliver effective cognitive and behavioural therapy for people with depression and with anxiety disorders*. London: Department of Health.

3

MI theory

This chapter will start by exploring the role of theory generally within therapeutic practice. It will move on to consider the emergence of MI theory, before beginning to describe the potential contribution of its application within MICBT practice.

In order to explore the issue of MI theory, it is first worth revisiting what the term 'theory' actually means. *The Oxford English Dictionary* (2019) offers two definitions:

1. A set of principles on which the practice of an activity is based
2. An idea used to account for a situation or justify a course of action

There are also many academic definitions of theory. Klee (1997) proposed that "theory is an attempt to organize the facts – some 'proven', some more conjectural – within a domain of inquiry into a structurally coherent system" (p. 12), while Wong (2018) suggested: "Theories are more than just guesses, because they have to be at the very least partially supported by some facts or data" and "almost all of our theories are partial and so to make advances we do often need to conjecture". These descriptions are intended to help consider the basis for theory–practice links, as well as to examine both MI and CBT as therapeutic modalities.

Finding a coherent theory to explain MI's effectiveness was not initially a priority (Miller, 1999). Indeed de Almeida Neto (2017) suggested that the delivery of MI across diverse contexts has been based on evidence of MI's effectiveness, in the absence of an integrative theoretical basis. A recent theoretical development was proposed by de Almeida Neto (2017), who drew on evolutionary theory as a way of explaining why MI supports behaviour change, proposing that a lack of resistance to change advocated by others communicates messages about social dominance and submissiveness within a group. While individuals influenced by others may be seen as "pushovers", social rank is maintained through the concept of psychological reactance. Because MI supports client autonomy, it potentially provides a non-threatening environment in terms of social hierarchy.

Adherence to this theoretical perspective has important issues for practitioners of CBT. Acknowledging that clients may be essentially 'pre-programmed' to resist ideas of change imposed by others and even to perceive these as a social threat highlights the importance of creating a therapeutic culture that fosters autonomous decision-making and promotes a partnership between the therapist and client, in which responsibility for change is acknowledged as being within the client's domain. These ideas, while central to the spirit of MI (Miller & Rollnick, 2013), are not necessarily explicit within CBT.

However, while de Almeida Neto (2017) offered an explanation for *why* MI works, this does not necessarily address the first dictionary definition of theory as "a set of principles on which the practice of an activity is based" (*Oxford English Dictionary*, 2019). Atkinson and Woods (2017) suggested that repeated changes to MI's central structure have meant that it lacks theoretical stability, leading to diverse and poorly defined practice. However, there is ongoing interest in the theoretical development of MI, and Miller and Rose (2009) ignited interest not only in underpinning theory, but in the mechanisms of MI, which help to make it effective by proposing an emergent theory of MI, based around the idea that it had two specific components:

- Relational skills: including empathy and attention to the elements of the MI spirit (acceptance, compassion, evocation and partnership)

- Technical components: which involve evoking and strengthening change talk.

These will be explored further in Chapter 12.

While relatively limited attention has since been paid to this potentially important notion, certainly in terms of a theoretical perspective for guiding practice (Miller & Rollnick, 2013), conceptually this is to date the most coherent and explicit framework for understanding MI. The idea of relational factors being important has empirical backing (e.g. Asay & Lambert, 1999) and the idea of a therapeutic alliance being of central importance is increasingly commonplace. Arguably, MI provides a more accurate description of relational factors than other therapeutic approaches including CBT through defining the spirit, and also implicitly through advocating use of specific therapeutic (OARS) skills (see Chapters 21–24). However, while the idea of relational factors may be important as a theory, it still lacks definition. For example, Moyers and Miller (2013) recently highlighted the central importance of empathy within MI, yet it is no longer a key feature of the central components (processes, skills, spirit) and instead is arguably less visible than in the previous editions of MI (Miller & Rollnick, 1991; 2002).

There are arguments for and against strengthening MI theory which also have implications for MICBT practice. In terms of advantages, MI is contemporary and current, building on iterative practitioner feedback. However, its lack of theoretical stability may mean it may be difficult to learn, with implications for training, proficiency and fidelity. Additionally, descriptions of MI might encompass a range of practices, and there may be a lack of empirical rationale for theory and practice developments (Atkinson & Woods, 2017).

The next chapter considers the possible advantages of understanding MICBT within the context of some of the motivational theories which led to MI's inception, particularly considering how understanding these could potentially strengthen MICBT practice. It will also argue that despite its lack of theoretical attention, the roots of MI are informed strongly by motivational theory.

Summary

1. The term theory relates both to the underlying organising idea and the principles which guide practice.
2. Evolutionary theory offers an explanation as to why MI works, by highlighting the importance of resistance in social dominance theory. Compliance to pressure from others potentially undermines social status, and this may mitigate against behavioural change.
3. Coherent theory guiding MI practice is still emerging. A useful theoretical perspective may involve paying attention to the relational and technical components of MI.
4. Theoretical development may have both advantages and disadvantages to MICBT practice.

References

Asay, T. P., & Lambert, M. J. (1999). The empirical case for the common factors in therapy: Quantitative findings. In M. A. Hubble, S. D. Miller, & B. L. Duncan (Eds.), *The heart and soul of change: What works in therapy* (pp. 23–55). Washington, DC: American Psychological Association.

Atkinson, C., & Woods, K. (2017). Establishing theoretical stability and treatment integrity for motivational interviewing. *Behavioural and Cognitive Psychotherapy*, *45*(4), 337–350. doi:10.1017/S1352465817000145

de Almeida Neto, A. C. (2017). Understanding motivational interviewing: An evolutionary perspective. *Evolutionary Psychological Science*, *3*, 379–389. doi:10.1007/s40806-017-0096-6

Klee, R. (1997). *Introduction to the philosophy of science. Cutting nature at its seams*. New York: Oxford University Press.

Miller, W. R. (1999). Toward a theory of MI. *Motivational Interviewing Newsletter: Updates, Education and Training (MINUET)*, *6.3*(September). Retrieved from http://www.motivationalinterview.net/clinical/theory.html

Miller, W. R., & Rollnick, S. (1991). *Motivational interviewing: Preparing people to change addictive behaviour*. New York: Guilford Press.

Miller, W. R., & Rollnick, S. (2002). *Motivational interviewing, second edition: Preparing people for change*. New York: Guilford Press.

Miller, W. R., & Rollnick, S. (2013). *Motivational interviewing, third edition: Helping people change*. New York: Guilford Press.

Miller, W. R., & Rose, G. S. (2009). Toward a theory of motivational interviewing. *The American Psychologist, 64*(6), 527–537. doi:10.1037/a0016830

Moyers, T. B., & Miller, W. R. (2013). Is low therapist empathy toxic? *Psychology of Addictive Behaviors, 27*(3), 878–884. doi:10.1037/a0030274

Oxford English Dictionary. (2019). *Oxford English Dictionary*. Retrieved May 28, 2019, from http://www.oed.com/

Wong, G. (2018). Making theory from knowledge syntheses useful for public health. *International Journal of Public Health, 63*(5), 555–556. doi:10.1007/s00038-018-1098-2

4

The implications of theory for MICBT practice

In the preceding chapter, we explored MI theory in general terms and its implications for MICBT practice. This chapter will focus on why theory might actually be important in promoting effective outcomes for clients. It will revisit the theory which prompted the emergence of MI, considering why this was felt necessary, and look at implications for MICBT. Finally, it will look at links between MI and CBT theory and discuss how integration might strengthen both approaches, from a theoretical perspective.

The contribution of theory to therapeutic practice

Dalgetty, Miller and Dombrowski (2019) investigated the claim that theory use leads to more effective behaviour change intervention by analysing published systematic literature reviews. While their findings did not necessarily suggest that theory use improved effectiveness per se, there was promising evidence from studies involving MI or self-determination theory (SDT) (see Chapter 6) for physical activity and/or dietary interventions. Specifically, Samdal, Eide, Barth, Williams and Meland (2017) found that among their 48 included studies, those that included client-centred approaches and autonomy support, informed by MI and SDT, produced better lasting effects.

In the past, Miller (2017) has acknowledged criticism of a lack of theoretical explanation of the efficacy of MI but insisted that theory development has not been a priority (cf. Miller & Rollnick, 2012).

What is interesting in the work of Dalgetty et al. (2019) and Samdal et al. (2017) is that MI in itself is considered as a theory of change. From this perspective, we argue that theory is at the very heart of MI and that understanding the theory which sits at its core can help enhance motivation within CBT.

We will next revisit the very first published article on MI (Miller, 1983), exploring the theory which informed its original development.

The theoretical basis of MI

In the very first published description of MI, Miller (1983) drew on theories of attribution, cognitive dissonance and self-efficacy in challenging traditional models of motivation in problem drinkers. What he observed were that attributions were frequently made that clients were "resistant" or "in denial" and would only comply with treatment once their lives were sufficiently unmanageable that they were required to accept treatment. Additionally, attributions for change were then linked to the characteristics of the therapist or treatment programme, rather than the strengths and resources of the client. MI places responsibility for change on the client, and indeed allocates credit for change to the client, thus promoting internal attribution. Robinson (2009) addresses this process when discussing the client's theory of change. Specifically, this means that, rather than having to accommodate the therapist's theory of change, the client's views about change are central, and therapy is tailored around these.

Dobson (2007) noted that, within CBT, while resistance is often characterised as problematic, the key to addressing it is an effective working alliance. Taking this a step further, Miller (1983) conceptualised motivation, not as a personality characteristic, but as an interpersonal process within which motivational principles, such as internal attribution, cognitive dissonance and self-efficacy need to be incorporated.

How can incorporating MI into CBT help, from a theoretical perspective

Through skilful practice, MI can help promote cognitive dissonance (see Chapter 9) where the client recognises a discrepancy between current patterns of behaviour and either their values and core beliefs, or their preferred future. Additionally there are links between internal attribution and self-efficacy theory (Bandura, 1997) – the extent to which clients believe themselves to be capable of behaviour change (see also Chapter 9) – and locus of control theory (Rotter, 1966) which considers the extent to which events are perceived to be within a client's control. Given evidence that addressing motivation is an important mechanism in the effectiveness of MI (see Chapter 11), an understanding of these theoretical principles may enhance practice within CBT.

Motivational principles within CBT

To the best of the authors' knowledge, most CBT practice is based on the work of Beck (1979). Therapists typically use this as a basis for their CBT models and many are rooted in the Beckian tradition. Arguably, typical CBT practice is a development of this tradition, based on empirical research.

Assessment of, and attention to, a client's motivation to change is arguably lacking within CBT theory and practice. Roth and Pilling (2007), for example, only mention motivation briefly, in relation to readiness for psychological intervention. Dalgetty et al. (2019) suggested that CBT was not as theoretically robust as MI, and indeed that it may be derived from cognitive theories which are now considerably old, such as cognitive theories of the 1960s and 1970s, and the work of Albert Ellis in deriving rational emotive behavioural therapy (Dobson, 2007). Miller and Rollnick (2009) recognised that the basis for MI was different from CBT in that it does not equip clients with something they are perceived to lack, or teach new skills. However, it also does not assume that the client believes that therapy would be in their best interest and/or is motivated towards change.

With these considerations in mind, the next three chapters (5–7) will consider three different theoretical perspectives from which MICBT and behaviour change might be explored – Rogerian counselling, SDT and the transtheoretical model. All of these theoretical perspectives have arguably been influential to the development of MI, and the chapters will consider, in turn, their potential contribution to MICBT practice.

Summary

1. There is some evidence to suggest that theory-based motivational approaches to therapy can improve intervention effectiveness.
2. Specifically addressing motivation, from a theoretical standpoint, might help improve the effectiveness of CBT.

References

Bandura, A. (1997). *Self-efficacy: The exercise of control*. Gordonsville, VA: Worth Publishers.

Beck, A. T. (1979). *Cognitive therapy of depression*. New York: Guilford Press.

Dalgetty, R., Miller, C. B., & Dombrowski, S. U. (2019). Examining the theory-effectiveness hypothesis: A systematic review of systematic reviews. *British Journal of Health Psychology*. doi:10.1111/bjhp.12356

Dobson, K. S. (Ed). (2007). *Handbook of cognitive-behavioral therapies*. 3rd edition. London: Guilford Press.

Miller, W. R. (1983). Motivational interviewing with problem drinkers. *Behavioural Psychotherapy*, *11*(2), 147–172. doi:10.1017/S01413 47300006583

Miller, W. R. (2017). *Taking the lower place: Motivational interviewing and social dominance*. Malahide, Ireland, October 5: 20th Anniversary Forum of the Motivational Interviewing Network of Trainers.

Miller, W. R., & Rollnick, S. (2009). Ten things that motivational interviewing is not. *Behavioural and Cognitive Psychotherapy*, *37*, 129–140. doi:10.1017/S1352465809005128

Miller, W. R., & Rollnick, S. (2012). Meeting in the middle: Motivational interviewing and self-determination theory. *The International Journal of Behavioral Nutrition and Physical Activity*, *9*, 25. doi:10.1186/1479-5868-9-25

Robinson, B. (2009). When therapist variables and the client's theory of change meet. *Psychotherapy I*, *15*(4), 60–65. doi:10.1002/cnm.3145

Roth, A. D., & Pilling, S. (2007). *The competences required to deliver effective cognitive and behavioural therapy for people with depression and with anxiety disorders*. London: Department of Health.

Rotter, J. B. (1966). Generalized expectancies for internal versus external control of reinforcement. *Psychological Monographs: General and Applied*, *80*(1), 1–28. Retrieved from https://psycnet.apa.org/doiLanding?doi=10.1037%2Fh0092976

Samdal, G. B., Eide, G. E., Barth, T., Williams, G., & Meland, E. (2017). Effective behaviour change techniques for physical activity and healthy eating in overweight and obese adults; systematic review and meta-regression analyses, *14*(42), 1–14. doi:10.1186/s12966-017-0494-y

5

MICBT and Rogerian counselling

Miller and Moyers (2017) recently reinforced how MI evolved from person-centred Rogerian counselling. Csillik (2013) proposed MI to be an evolution of the theory of Rogers (1959) which addresses motivational problems, suggesting that MI combines a client-centred, supportive and empathic counselling style with specific techniques. Csillik (2013) also identified that MI was intentionally briefer than person-centred counselling and more likely to focus on a specific objective.

This chapter will consider how Rogerian principles and approaches influenced MI and behaviour therapy in general. Furthermore, it will examine the inextricable links between MICBT and Rogerian counselling, with particular focus on the implications for the therapeutic relationship. Carl Rogers and others (e.g. Traux & Carkhuff, 1967) were pioneers of both process and outcome research in psychotherapy. We will explore this literature and the debate around what are often termed 'common' or 'non-specific' factors in therapy.

Rogers (1959) identified three core conditions of person-centred counselling: empathy, acceptance (including unconditional positive regard) and congruence. These conditions will now be considered in turn with reference to MICBT.

Empathy

Accurate empathy is part of the 'acceptance' component of MI spirit (see Chapter 8), although arguably it was more prominent in the previous versions of MI (e.g. Miller & Rollnick, 2002) when it appeared as a dimension of the then triadic spirit, in its own right.

Csillik (2013) highlighted that demonstrating empathy has been, and continues to be, a feature of MI proficiency assessment (e.g. Moyers, Rowell, Manuel, Ernst, & Houck, 2016). Moyers and Miller (2013) emphasised the importance of therapist empathy in relation to both client outcomes and avoiding harm.

Although not a specific focus of MI or CBT, also useful here are the notions of 'affective' and 'cognitive' empathy. Affective empathy is an observer's emotional response to the affective state of others. Cognitive empathy is the process of understanding another's perspective (Davis, 1983). The latter is helpful in therapy, while the former can be a hindrance. It is therefore helpful for MICBT practitioners to reflect on and evaluate their own empathic stance.

Acceptance

While the spirit component is considered more comprehensively in Chapter 8, it is worth comparing it briefly to Rogerian ideals of a positive, non-judgemental and accepting attitude, demonstrated through appreciation, non-possessive caring and unconditional positive regard (Csillik, 2013). The spirit of MI includes 'acceptance' as one of its core components, although its conceptualisation might be more multifaceted than when originally defined by Rogers (1959). The MI component of acceptance is comprised of four separate aspects: absolute worth, accurate empathy, affirmation and autonomy. Absolute worth is synonymous with recognising the potential and inherent worth of every client, as well as the Rogerian ideals detailed above. Within accurate empathy, there is crossover with the Rogerian empathy core component, while affirmation is about seeking and acknowledging the client's strengths, efforts and values (Miller & Rollnick, 2013). Finally, autonomy, previously a component of the spirit in its own right (Miller & Rollnick, 2002), refers to respecting the client's capacity for self-direction and freedom of choice (Miller & Rollnick, 2013).

Congruence

Congruence relates to the genuineness of the therapist within the therapeutic relationship, suggesting that they should be themselves, and aware of their attitudes and feelings towards the client. Csillik (2013) suggested that its impact on therapeutic outcomes had received less attention than the other two core conditions. While congruence has not been emphasised specifically within MI, there may be some parity with the compassion component of the spirit (see Chapter 8), where therapists are expected to act in the client's best interest, rather than for financial or entrepreneurial gain, or for personal or professional reward.

Common factors in therapy and implications for CBT practitioners

Roth and Pilling (2007) highlighted the importance of the "generic therapeutic competencies" required for effective CBT. However, their descriptions are at best notional and include "ability to engage client", "ability to manage emotional content of sessions" and "ability to foster and maintain a good therapeutic alliance and to grasp the client's perspective and 'world view'" (p. 12). Arguably, MI has gone a long way to offering much more substantial guidance around the 'general' or 'non-specific' factors in therapy, through its strong relational philosophy, based on Rogerian principles and the MI spirit. CBT is less clear in its definition of core interpersonal skills contributing to a therapeutic alliance within therapy, including elements relating to the philosophy and interpersonal skills of and therapeutic alliance within therapy (Driessen & Hollon, 2011). To this effect, CBT practitioners may benefit from reference to MI's delineation of the relational component of MI, based on empathy and interpersonal spirit (Miller & Rose, 2009, see also Chapter 12).

Summary

1. Rogerian principles have underpinned the development of MI practice.
2. Understanding the core conditions of person-centred counselling and the relational aspects of MI can be helpful to CBT practitioners, as factors relating to the therapeutic alliance are less well-defined within CBT.

References

Csillik, A. S. (2013). Understanding motivational interviewing effectiveness: Contributions from Rogers' client-centered approach. *Humanistic Psychologist*, *41*(4), 350–363. doi:10.1080/08873267.2013.779906

Davis, M. H. (1983). Measuring individual differences in empathy: Evidence for a multidimensional approach. *Journal of Personality and Social Psychology*, *44*(1), 113–126. doi:10.1037/0022-3514.44.1.113

Driessen, E., & Hollon, S. D. (2011). Motivational interviewing from a cognitive behavioral perspective. *Cognitive and Behavioral Practice*, *18*(1), 70–73. doi:10.1016/j.cbpra.2010.02.007

Miller, W. R., & Moyers, T. B. (2017). Motivational interviewing and the clinical science of Carl Rogers. *Journal of Consulting and Clinical Psychology*, *85*(8), 757–766. doi:10.1037/ccp0000179

Miller, W. R., & Rollnick, S. (2002). *Motivational interviewing, second edition: Preparing people for change*. New York: Guilford Press.

Miller, W. R., & Rollnick, S. (2013). *Motivational interviewing, third edition: Helping people change*. New York: Guilford Press.

Miller, W. R., & Rose, G. S. (2009). Toward a theory of motivational interviewing. *The American Psychologist*, *64*(6), 527–537. doi:10.1037/a0016830

Moyers, T. B., & Miller, W. R. (2013). Is low therapist empathy toxic? *Psychology of Addictive Behaviors*, *27*(3), 878–884. doi:10.1037/a0030274

Moyers, T. B., Rowell, L. N., Manuel, J. K., Ernst, D., & Houck, J. M. (2016). The Motivational Interviewing Treatment Integrity Code (MITI 4): Rationale, preliminary reliability and validity. *Journal of Substance Abuse Treatment*, *65*, 36–42. doi:10.1016/j.jsat.2016.01.001

Rogers, C. R. (1959). A theory of therapy, personality and interpersonal relationships as developed in the client-centred framework. In S. Koch (Ed.), *Psychology: The study of science (Vol. 3). Formulations of the person and the social context* (pp. 184–256). New York: McGraw-Hill.

Roth, A. D., & Pilling, S. (2007). *The competences required to deliver effective cognitive and behavioural therapy for people with depression and with anxiety disorders*. London: Department of Health.

Traux, C. B., & Carkhuff, R. R. (1967). *Toward effective counseling and psychotherapy*. Chicago: Aldine.

6

Self-determination theory and MICBT practice

MI and self-determination theory

One theory of motivation which aligns closely with MI is self-determination theory (SDT) (Ryan & Deci, 2000). Previously, Markland, Ryan, Tobin and Rollnick (2005) and Vansteenkiste and Sheldon (2006) proposed that SDT could potentially theoretically underpin MI. Although Miller and Rollnick (2012), recognising parallels between MI and SDT, did not pursue systematic integration, understanding the principles of SDT could potentially be a way of understanding, assessing and ultimately enhancing client motivation and capacity for change.

What does SDT say about motivation?

There are two main aspects to SDT: the motivational continuum and basic human needs. The motivational continuum challenges the traditional dichotomy of intrinsic and extrinsic motivation. Instead, it identifies a continuum of motivation with intrinsic motivation as something inherently enjoyable, at one end, and with amotivation, at the other. In between are degrees of extrinsic motivation within which behaviours are increasingly self-regulated and self-actualised (see Figure 6.1). For example, an individual advised to take up exercise for health reasons (external regulation) might start to see benefits from walking and incorporate it into a daily routine (introjected regulation). Motivation may be further enhanced through joining a walking

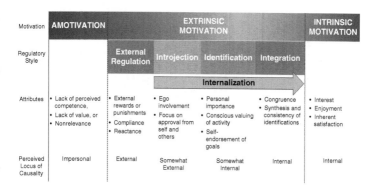

Motivation	AMOTIVATION	EXTRINSIC MOTIVATION				INTRINSIC MOTIVATION
Regulatory Style		External Regulation	Introjection	Identification	Integration	
		Internalization →				
Attributes	• Lack of perceived competence, • Lack of value, or • Nonrelevance	• External rewards or punishments • Compliance • Reactance	• Ego involvement • Focus on approval from self and others	• Personal importance • Conscious valuing of activity • Self-endorsement of goals	• Congruence • Synthesis and consistency of identifications	• Interest • Enjoyment • Inherent satisfaction
Perceived Locus of Causality	Impersonal	External	Somewhat External	Somewhat Internal	Internal	Internal

Figure 6.1 Self-determination theory's taxonomy of motivation

Note: From the Center for Self-determination Theory © 2017. Reproduced with permission.

group, bringing social and experiential, as well as health benefits (identified regulation). Ultimately, this could even lead to organising walks or membership of the walking group committee (integrated regulation).

In relation to the second aspect, SDT identifies three areas of human need – autonomy, competence and relatedness – all of which are important to motivation. Competence relates to feeling as if you can do something; autonomy to feeling as if you are in control of your own behaviour and outcomes; and relatedness to feeling as if people close to you and who matter to you are related to the behaviour.

To exemplify: a person whose drinking has become problematic will be unlikely to change until they take responsibility for managing their drinking (autonomy). In terms of competence, they also need to feel that they have the personal skills and resources to achieve this, which links to the MI principle of supporting self-efficacy (Miller & Rollnick, 2002, see Chapter 9). Finally, according to the need for relatedness, motivation to change is likely to be enhanced if the change (in this case managing drinking) is valued by people important to the individual.

What can SDT offer MICBT?

In order to answer this question, we will first consider the motivational continuum and then the three core human needs. In relation to the motivational continuum, Miller and Rollnick (2002) used intrinsic motivation as a way of describing a prerequisite for change. Ryan and Deci's (2000) SDT offers a more sophisticated framework for how motivation can be developed and increasingly internalised. In many cases, the clients Miller and Rollnick initially tried to reach with MI were towards the 'not self-determined' end of the continuum, and if motivated at all were externally regulated, for example to avoid the break-up of a relationship or a criminal conviction, rather than valuing behaviour change for personal reasons. Vansteenkiste and Sheldon (2006) proposed that MI is about trying to successfully promote the internalisation of extrinsic change intentions and also talked about the quality of the motivation, appreciating that change in relation to external factors, such as the avoidance of sanctions, might not be sustainable. Within MICBT it is important, within the notion of a motivational continuum, to consider how meaningful and important change is to a client and how this can be continually revisited and developed over time.

In terms of the three human needs, these potentially provide a useful framework for assessing motivation at the outset. Although motivation is clearly important in therapy, assessment and building of motivation do not appear to be central to CBT theory and practice (e.g. Roth & Pilling, 2007). The integration of SDT and MI principles into CBT may be a very specific way of enhancing practice. In terms of considering autonomy, it may be useful to assess the extent to which the client perceives themselves to have responsibility for change, or whether it is something which has arisen because the behaviour has become problematic for others. Competence can be assessed through discussions with the client and potentially developed through skills-based training (e.g. assertiveness training, social skills). Finally, auditing what Prochaska, Norcross and DiClemente (1994) described as "helping relationships" which could include familial or peer relationships, or self-help groups (see also Chapter 29), would be a good way of understanding how relatedness factors might affect motivation to change.

In relation to all three needs, understanding motivation could usefully be incorporated into CBT formulation, which could then be used to guide intervention (Roth & Pilling, 2007).

MICBT and SDT in practice

A practical example of integrating MICBT with SDT is provided by Britton, Patrick, Wenzel and Williams (2011) who exemplified use of the combined approaches for clients with suicidal ideation. Specifically, the authors highlighted that motivation to live is key to prevention, and yet many individuals considering suicide are ambivalent: "they want to die, but they also want to live with less pain" (p. 17). In Britton et al.'s (2011) practice description, three phases were suggested:

- Phase 1: Exploring the presenting problem and motivation (in this case, to die)
- Phase 2: Building the motivation (in this case, to live)
- Phase 3: Strengthening commitment (to live)

In the example given, MI approaches are used as a precursor to a CBT intervention.

Summary

SDT can potentially provide an underpinning theoretical framework for MICBT, with practical implications. Specifically:

1. The motivational continuum can be used as a conceptual framework to assess, develop and evaluate client motivation.

2. CBT practice can be enhanced by specific consideration of motivational factors.
3. The three SDT human needs (autonomy, competence and relatedness) should be considered within CBT case formulation.
4. Britton et al.'s (2011) practice description may offer guidance for incorporating SDT within MICBT.

References

Britton, P. C., Patrick, H., Wenzel, A., & Williams, G. C. (2011). Integrating motivational interviewing and self-determination theory with cognitive behavioral therapy to prevent suicide. *Cognitive and Behavioral Practice*, *18*(1), 16–27. doi:10.1016/j.cbpra.2009.06.004

Markland, D., Ryan, R. M., Tobin, V. J., & Rollnick, S. (2005). Motivational interviewing and self-determination theory. *Journal of Social and Clinical Psychology*, *24*, 811–831. doi:10.1521/jscp.2005.24.6.811

Miller, W. R., & Rollnick, S. (2002). *Motivational interviewing, second Edition: Preparing people for change*. New York: Guilford Press.

Miller, W. R., & Rollnick, S. (2012). Meeting in the middle: Motivational interviewing and self-determination theory. *The International Journal of Behavioral Nutrition and Physical Activity*, *9*, 25. doi:10.1186/1479-5868-9-25

Prochaska, J. O., Norcross, J. C., & DiClemente, C. C. (1994). *Changing for good: A revolutionary six-stage program for overcoming bad habits and moving your life positively forward*. New York: Quill.

Roth, A. D., & Pilling, S. (2007). *The competences required to deliver effective cognitive and behavioural therapy for people with depression and with anxiety disorders*. London: Department of Health.

Ryan, R. M., & Deci, E. L. (2000). Intrinsic and extrinsic motivations: Classic definitions and new directions. *Contemporary Educational Psychology*, *25*(1), 54–67.

Vansteenkiste, M., & Sheldon, K. M. (2006). There's nothing more practical than a good theory: Integrating motivational interviewing and self-determination theory. *The British Journal of Clinical Psychology*, *45*(1), 63–82.

7

MICBT and the transtheoretical model

The relationship between MI and the transtheoretical model

Initial research on the transtheoretical model of therapy (TTM) (Prochaska & DiClemente, 1982) compared 18 leading therapy systems and over 300 therapy outcomes (Prochaska, 1979) in an attempt to establish common processes by which therapy helped people to change. From this emerged the model of stages of change (see Figures 7.1 and 7.2), supported by empirical evidence comparing self-reports of smoking behaviour change (DiClemente & Prochaska, 1982). The model proposes that people potentially pass through a series of stages when changing their behaviour. It is acknowledged that its original two-dimensional presentation (Figure 7.1) implying a linear progression through the stages may be over-simplistic and that motivation to change – complex, variable and iterative – might be better represented by a three-dimensional spiral (Figure 7.2).

MI and the TTM emerged at around the same time, and in the first edition of *Motivational Interviewing* (Miller & Rollnick, 1991), the model of stages of change was proposed as useful in making assessments about client readiness for change and guiding practice. However, by the time MI was redefined in the second edition (Miller & Rollnick, 2002), the TTM had become much more peripheral, with overlaps between the TTM and MI presented in a contributed chapter (DiClemente & Velasquez, 2002). Later, perhaps as a result of high-profile criticism of the

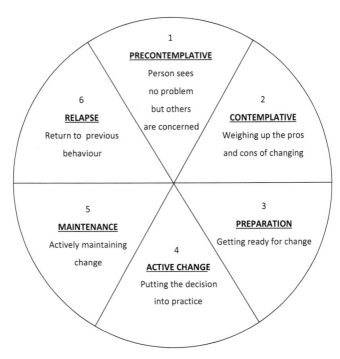

Figure 7.1 Two-dimensional representation of the model of stages of change

TTM (e.g. West, 2005), Miller and Rollnick (2009) clarified that "MI is not based on the transtheoretical model" (p. 130).

Some argued that it was too late! Atkinson and Amesu (2007) had previously noted that within educational settings, MI and the TTM were often used simultaneously and (McNamara, 2014) went further, stating, "In my opinion, attempts to 'roll back' the integration of the TTM and MI are akin to Canute attempting to reverse the incoming movement of the tide" (p. 242). While the TTM is not now visible in core literature (Miller & Rollnick, 2013), its legacy remains within both the mechanisms through which MI is effective (Copeland, McNamara, Kelson, & Simpson, 2015) and contemporary practice (e.g. Bortolon et al., 2017).

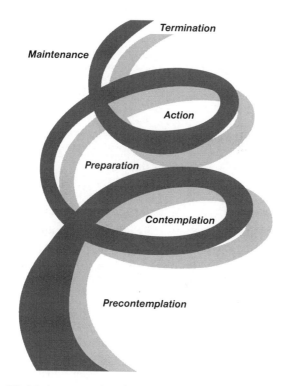

Figure 7.2 Spiral representation of the model of stages of change

The TTM as a practice heuristic for MI

Atkinson and Woods (2017) highlighted that the TTM is not a theory and has no explanatory power suggesting instead that, due to its centrality to the emergence of MI, it may have become a useful heuristic for guiding practitioners on both the pace and focus of therapy. Both the MI and the TTM acknowledge that responsibility for change lies with the client and that the ultimate goal involves resolving ambivalence and supporting positive lifestyle changes. Atkinson (2014) suggested that the visual structure of the TTM might help make the underlying MI concept of ambivalence about change more accessible to practitioners and may also improve client agency in terms of improving personal understanding of change, particularly in terms of normalising relapse.

The application of the TTM within MICBT

Squires (2014) described how that the TTM could be used a triage tool for assessing whether CBT might be an appropriate intervention, proposing that it was likely to be most effective where the client recognised a need for change. Describing the approach in the context of working with young people in schools, Squires (2014) suggested that a systemic response, in this case the teacher or school taking a different approach, would be appropriate for those not ready, or not seeing the need for change (precontemplative); with MI the most appropriate approach for young people ambivalent (contemplative) about change.

Another example is provided by Kamen (2009) who offered a systematic practitioner structure, defining therapist behaviours at each stage of change and improving client agency through the use of a TTM-related mnemonic (revive, value, ready, get-set, go). Kamen (2009) suggested that this TTM-based structure could guide the timing of CBT-informed exposure with response prevention, for children and adolescents vulnerable to non-suicidal self-injury.

Advantages and disadvantages of using the TTM within MI

Some of the advantages and disadvantages of using the TTM as a conceptual model to guide MICBT practice are listed in Table 7.1.

Table 7.1 Advantages and disadvantages of using the TTM to support MI

Advantages	*Disadvantages*
• Considering readiness to change may be an important mechanism in client outcomes (see Chapter 11). • The TTM provides a tangible, visual and potentially accessible heuristic for both clients and therapists. • The TTM potentially allows more sophisticated consideration of the rather nebulous concept of ambivalence. • There is potential for progress review through use of the TTM. Furthermore, in terms of outcomes, it allows for detection of more subtle changes in client behaviour, rather than solely tangible behavioural change.	• The TTM is not MI, nor part of MI, and presenting them as synonymous could cause confusion. • The TTM could potentially detract from the core elements of MI: the spirit, processes and skills. • Change is often non-linear and the TTM is over-simplistic and potentially unrepresentative. • Preoccupation with readiness for and/or the stages of change, may lead to the inappropriate, or inequitable allocation of resources.

Specifically with MICBT, MI is sometimes seen as a precursor to behavioural interventions, including CBT. While it is useful to acknowledge that MI skills and processes could be useful in engaging the client, and in evoking change talk, there is a risk that in seeing the two approaches taking place at different stages of readiness (e.g. MI during precontemplation and contemplation; CBT at preparation), the potential strengths of both approaches are not fully utilised in supporting the client. Indeed, using a more integrated and responsive approach allows therapists to simultaneously use both approaches in promoting client change. In research by Iarussi, Tyler, Crawford and Crawford (2016), therapists using an integrated MICBT approach identified a number of themes associated with readiness for change. These suggested that within their practice, that therapists

- identify what is needed in the therapeutic relationship and then respond to meet those needs;
- assess client readiness and motivation to change, and then match their responses to meet clients in the process of change and assist them towards change;
- identify client speech that suggests problematic thinking or a need for change and then use CBT methods when clients are determined to be ready to change.

Summary

West's (2005) criticisms of the TTM centre on a practitioner's over-reliance on its structure, leading to poor assessment and intervention practice. However, as part of client-centred, reflective MICBT practice, we believe that the TTM can

1. act as a heuristic for guiding practice and deciding when (if at all) it might be most appropriate to use CBT;
2. have an educative function as a heuristic, improving client agency and normalising relapse;
3. generate a deeper understanding of the nuances and degrees of ambivalence amongst practitioners.

References

Atkinson, C. (2014). Motivational interviewing and the transtheoretical model. In E. McNamara (Ed.), *Motivational interviewing: Further applications with children and young people* (pp. 19–32). Ainsdale: PBM.

Atkinson, C., & Amesu, M. (2007). Using solution-focused approaches in motivational interviewing with young people. *Pastoral Care in Education*, *25*(June), 31–37. doi:10.1111/j.1468-0122.2007.00405.x

Atkinson, C., & Woods, K. (2017). Establishing theoretical stability and treatment integrity for motivational interviewing. *Behavioural and Cognitive Psychotherapy*, *45*(4), 337–350. doi:10.1017/S1352 465817000145

Bortolon, C. B., Moreira, T. D. C., Signor, L., Guahyba, B. L., Figueiró, L. R., Ferigolo, M., & Barros, H. M. T. (2017). Six-month outcomes of a randomized, motivational tele-intervention for change in the codependent behavior of family members of drug users. *Substance Use & Misuse*, *52*, 164–174. doi:10.1080/1082608 4.2016.1223134

Copeland, L., McNamara, R., Kelson, M., & Simpson, S. (2015). Mechanisms of change within motivational interviewing in relation to health behaviors outcomes: A systematic review. *Patient Education and Counseling*, *98*(4), 401–411. doi:10.1016/j. pec.2014.11.022

DiClemente, C. C. Prochaska, J. O. (1982). Self change and therapy change of smoking behavior: A comparison of processes of change in cessation and maintenance. *Addictive Behaviours*, *7*, 133–142.

Iarussi, M. M., Tyler, J. M., Crawford, S. H., & Crawford, C. V. (2016). Counselor training in two evidence-based practices: Motivational interviewing and cognitive behavior therapy. *The Journal of Counselor Preparation and Supervision*, 8(3). doi:10.7729/83.1113

Kamen, D. (2009). Stop our children from hurting themselves? Stages of change, motivational interviewing, and exposure therapy applications for non-suicidal self-injury in children. *International Journal of Behavioral Consultation & Therapy*, *5*(1), 106–123.

McNamara, E. (2014). *Motivational interviewing: Further applications with children and young people.* Ainsdale: Positive Behaviour Management.

Miller, W. R., & Rollnick, S. (1991). *Motivational interviewing: Preparing people to change addictive behaviour*. New York: Guilford Press.

Miller, W. R., & Rollnick, S. (2002). *Motivational interviewing, second edition: Preparing people for change*. New York: Guilford Press.

Miller, W. R., & Rollnick, S. (2013). *Motivational interviewing, third edition: Helping people change*. New York: Guilford Press.

Prochaska, J. O. (1979). *Systems in psychotherapy. A transtheoretical analysis*. Homewood, IL: Dorsey Press.

Prochaska, J. O., & DiClemente, C. C. (1982). Transtheoretical therapy: Toward a more integrative model of change. *Psychotherapy: Theory Research and Practice*, *19*(3), 276–288.

Squires, G. (2014). Motivational interviewing and cognitive behavioural therapy. In E. McNamara (Ed.), *Motivational interviewing: Further applications with children and young people* (pp. 193–205). Ainsdale: PBM.

West, R. (2005). Time for a change: Putting the transtheoretical (Stages of Change) model to rest. *Addiction*, *100*(8), 1036–1039.

8

The Spirit of MI

At the heart of MI, as defined by Miller and Rollnick (2013), are three core features – the spirit, the processes and the skills. The processes and skills will be more closely examined in the second section of this book, but the spirit – central to the core philosophy of MI – will be considered first, as it effectively underpins MI and the position from which it should be delivered.

Rollnick and Miller (1995) offered one of the first references to the spirit of MI, proposing that MI was based on seven core features, relating to ideas about eliciting motivation for and ideas about change from the client, while avoiding direct persuasion and working in partnership. By 2002, Miller and Rollnick had refined the spirit to a triadic philosophy, based on autonomy, collaboration and evocation; and most recently, what Miller and Rollnick (2013) referred to as "the set of heart and mind with which one enters the practice of MI" (p. 15) was presented as a four-aspect model, as shown in Figure 8.1.

Miller and Rollnick (2013) recognised the therapeutic relationship as a partnership and described MI as "an active collaboration between experts" (p. 15) involving the counsellor in guiding the process adeptly, and the client in knowing their own situation best. *Acceptance* is a rather more complex and multifaceted component, comprising four elements, as shown in Figure 8.2, which very much reference Rogerian principles (see Chapter 4). Collectively these encourage an approach in which the client's situation is viewed empathically and non-judgementally; where their responsibility and capacity for change is recognised; and where strengths, efforts and personal characteristics are recognised and valued.

Figure 8.1 The spirit of MI (Miller & Rollnick, 2013)

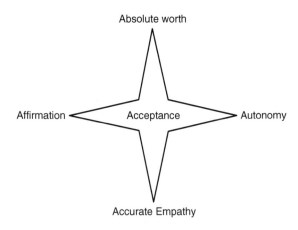

Figure 8.2 The four aspects of acceptance (Miller & Rollnick, 2013)

The recently added component of *compassion* (Miller & Rollnick, 2013) represents the intention that MI should always be used ethically and in the best interests of the client. Finally *evocation* acknowledges the concept of ambivalence and defines the counsellor's task as being to evoke and strengthen motivation for change.

Miller and Rollnick (2009), in redefining some of the key principles of MI within clinical practice, advocated for greater emphasis on the underlying spirit of MI, which they linked to Rogers's (1959) "critical conditions for change". The next section will explore the contribution understanding and practising the MI spirit can make to effective and client-centred CBT.

The spirit of MI and CBT

In exploring MI from a CBT perspective, Driessen and Hollon (2011) recognised the benefits of making the notion of ambivalence about change explicit within CBT practice. The authors highlighted that while CBT done well can be entirely consistent with MI, the fact is that MI is much more explicit about how demonstration of the spirit can support clients who are ambivalent. The benefits of being mindful of the MI spirit were evident in a study conducted by Kertes, Westra, Angus and Marcus (2011) in which some clients experiencing generalised anxiety disorder were offered MI as a precursor to CBT, while others were just offered MI. Those who had the MI 'pretreatment' tended to describe the CBT therapist as more collaborative and evocative, while CBT-only therapists were thought to be more directive. While the study was not without its limitations, the findings led Driessen and Hollon (2011) to conclude that "At the very least, it seems to us that training in MI would be a good supplement that would help therapists learn to do CBT in the spirit in which we were trained to do" (p. 71).

In terms of the therapeutic competencies specified by Roth and Pilling (2007), it is arguable that incorporating the spirit of

MI into CBT would allow a greater level of precision and reflection within somewhat nebulous CBT competencies relating to engaging the client, fostering and maintaining the therapeutic alliance and understanding the client's perspective. Attention to the specific components of the spirit (as defined in Figures 8.1 and 8.2) allows for more systematic and informed reflection on aspects which not only potentially address ambivalence about change but are arguably fundamental to the therapeutic alliance.

Atkinson and Woods (2018) proposed a series of prompts allowing practitioners to consider adherence to the spirit. In the following examples (see Table 8.1), therapists could reflect on the extent to which their practice is consistent with the statements.

Table 8.1 Statements to enable practitioner reflection on the spirit of MI

Spirit component	Reflective statements
Collaboration	• I have recognised that the client is the expert in knowing what is best for them. • I have shown that the work I do with the client represents a partnership.
Acceptance	• I have recognised that it is up to the client to make decisions about change. • I have attempted to identify the client's strengths. • I have been respectful of the client's needs.

Compassion	I have demonstrated:
	  ○ feelings of warmth and caring for the client
	  ○ an active commitment to meeting the client's needs.

Evocation	• I have tried to elicit reasons for change from the client. • I have understood that attempts at direct persuasion may be counterproductive. • I have listened carefully for change talk.

Summary

1. The spirit of MI represents its underlying philosophy and is defined by four components: collaboration, acceptance, compassion and evocation.
2. Implementation of the MI spirit may enhance CBT practice and allow for more explicit consideration of the spirit components in both addressing ambivalence and creating an effective therapeutic alliance.

References

Atkinson, C., & Woods, K. (2018). Integrity in the delivery of school-based motivational interviewing: Protocols for practitioners. In Mc-Namara, E. (Ed.), *Motivational interviewing with children and young people III: Education and community settings* (pp. 76–92). Ainsdale: Positive Behaviour Management.

Driessen, E., & Hollon, S. D. (2011). Motivational interviewing from a cognitive behavioral perspective. *Cognitive and Behavioral Practice*, *18*(1), 70–73. doi:10.1016/j.cbpra.2010.02.007

Kertes, A., Westra, H. A., Angus, L., & Marcus, M. (2011). The impact of motivational interviewing on client experiences of cognitive behavioral therapy for generalized anxiety disorder. *Cognitive and Behavioral Practice*, *18*(1), 55–69. doi:10.1016/j.cbpra. 2009.06.005

Miller, W. R., & Rollnick, S. (2002). *Motivational interviewing, second edition: Preparing people for change*. New York: Guilford Press.

Miller, W. R., & Rollnick, S. (2009). Ten things that motivational interviewing is not. *Behavioural and Cognitive Psychotherapy*, *37*, 129–140. doi:10.1017/S1352465809005128

Miller, W. R., & Rollnick, S. (2013). *Motivational interviewing: Helping people change*. 3rd edition. New York: Guilford Press.

Rogers, C. R. (1959). A theory of therapy, personality and interpersonal relationships as developed in the client-centred framework. In S. Koch (Ed.), *Psychology: The study of science (Vol. 3). Formulations of the person and the social context* (pp. 184–256). New York: McGraw-Hill.

Rollnick, S., & Miller, W. R. (1995). What is motivational interviewing? *Behavioural and Cognitive Psychotherapy*, *23*, 325–334. doi:10.1017/S135246580001643X

Roth, A. D., & Pilling, S. (2007). *The competences required to deliver effective cognitive and behavioural therapy for people with depression and with anxiety disorders*. London: Department of Health.

9

The Principles of MI

In the most recent delineation of MI (Miller & Rollnick, 2013), the authors replaced the principles, which had been previously at the heart of MI theory, with the processes (see Chapters 17–20). Reasons for this are not entirely clear (Atkinson & Woods, 2017), but it is possible that including another dimension to the existing core elements – the spirit, processes and skills – might be deemed to add further complexity to an approach which had already been recognised as difficult to learn (Miller & Rollnick, 2009). Nevertheless, we believe, particularly from a theoretical perspective, that understanding and enacting the principles of MI helps therapists undertake MI in accordance with its spirit (see Chapter 8) as well as offering specific operational guidance for using MI.

When described originally by Miller and Rollnick (1991), there were five principles of MI: express empathy, develop discrepancy, avoid argumentation, roll with resistance and support self-efficacy. Later 'avoid argumentation' was removed (Miller & Rollnick, 2002), and while no specific reason was given, this may have been due to the fact that this was implicit from the other principles, and because of increasing focus on avoiding the righting reflex (see Chapter 16). In the following sections, the four remaining principles defined by Miller and Rollnick (2002) will be explored in more detail.

Express empathy

We have already examined, in Chapters 4 and 8, just how important accurate empathy is to effective MI practice. Specifically, Miller and Rollnick (2002) described how paradoxically acceptance, which underlies accurate empathy, promotes change because the therapist understands and communicates that ambivalence is normal, through the therapeutic alliance.

Develop discrepancy

Miller and Rollnick (2002) reported that this principle borrowed its concept from Festinger's (1957) theory of cognitive dissonance. Specifically, this relates to a discrepancy between the client's current situation and their preferred future, and the psychological discomfort that can accompany this. For example, if a heavy drinker's preferred future is to maintain her career and her relationship, the point at which this is which this is put in jeopardy might be the point at which she starts to think about change. Miller and Rollnick (2002) noted "that change is motivated by perceived discrepancy between present behaviour and important personal goals or values" (p. 39) but that arguments for change should come from the client. While cognitive dissonance is identified and operationalised in MI, this is not generally the case in CBT.

Roll with resistance

This principle links to Miller and Rollnick's (2013) idea of ambivalence being like having a committee in your head, simultaneously arguing for and against change and thus rendering direct persuasion ineffective (see Chapter 2). To illustrate rolling with resistance, Miller and Rollnick (2002) used the metaphor of a martial artist utilising the attacker's momentum and bodyweight, rather than trying to defend it. Although the authors emphasised that MI is not a competition, exploiting the client's momentum for resisting change will paradoxically lead them into opportunities for self-change talk, or for finding their own solutions, as they can follow their own line of thinking and have no need to defend their position.

Rolling with resistance links to Bem's (1967) self-perception theory, which proposed that individuals come to know their own attitudes by inferring them from observations of their own behaviour. If clients are therefore allowed to explore their behaviour with the therapist without fear of judgement or reproach, they are in a better position to examine their own behaviour and, should they wish to, find reasons and opportunities for change.

Support self-efficacy

The final principle, self-efficacy, emerged from the work of Bandura (1997) who defined it as follows: "Perceived self-efficacy is concerned not with the number of skills you have, but with what you believe you can do with what you have under a variety of circumstances" (p. 37). In other words, self-efficacy relates to the confidence you have in relation to a specific task, and in MI terms, in relation to behaviour change. For example, a person who is very overweight may want to become slimmer but not believe that they are capable of doing so. Miller and Rollnick (2002) recognised that belief in one's ability to change is a powerful factor in motivation. They also proposed that this would be affected by the therapist's expectations about the client's capacity for change and the likelihood for change, even suggesting that these could represent a "self-fulfilling prophecy" (p. 41). In the third edition of *Motivational Interviewing,* Miller and Rollnick (2013) devoted 18 pages to "evoking hope and confidence", which relate directly to self-efficacy, indicating the continuing importance of this theoretical concept within MI.

The principles of MI, and MICBT

None of the principles of MI are referred to directly by Roth and Pilling (2007), although arguably they are implicit in competencies such as "ability to engage client", ability to "grasp the client's perspective and 'world view'" and "ability to identify and help the client modify core beliefs" (p. 17). While it is recognised that the philosophy of CBT recognises that clients should be active participants in therapy (Roth & Pilling, 2007), with the last of these, MI would potentially place more responsibility on the client to identify and modify beliefs through using the principles, with the view to strengthening both personal motivation and responsibility for change.

Summary

1. Although the four principles of MI – express empathy, develop discrepancy, roll with resistance and support self-efficacy – are no longer part of central MI theory, we believe they are both relevant and important to MICBT practice today.
2. Specific consideration and operationalisation of these principles is likely to enhance CBT practice, particularly for clients who are ambivalent or at an early stage of readiness for change.

References

Atkinson, C., & Woods, K. (2017). Establishing theoretical stability and treatment integrity for motivational interviewing. *Behavioural and Cognitive Psychotherapy*, *45*(4), 337–350. doi:10.1017/S1352465817000145

Bandura, A. (1997). *Self-efficacy: The exercise of control*. Gordonsville, VA: Worth Publishers.

Bem, D. J. (1967). Self-perception: An alternative interpretation of cognitive dissonance phenomena. *Psychological Review*, *74*(3), 183–200.

Festinger, L. A. (1957). *A theory of cognitive dissonance*. Stanford, CA: Stanford University Press.

Miller, W. R., & Rollnick, S. (1991). *Motivational interviewing: Preparing people to change addictive behaviour*. New York: Guilford Press.

Miller, W. R., & Rollnick, S. (2002). *Motivational interviewing, second edition: Preparing people for change.* New York: Guilford Press.

Miller, W. R., & Rollnick, S. (2009). Ten things that motivational interviewing is not. *Behavioural and Cognitive Psychotherapy, 37,* 129–140. doi:10.1017/S1352465809005128

Miller, W. R., & Rollnick, S. (2013). *Motivational interviewing, third edition: Helping people change.* New York: Guilford Press.

Roth, A. D., & Pilling, S. (2007). *The competences required to deliver effective cognitive and behavioural therapy for people with depression and with anxiety disorders.* London: Department of Health.

10

Evidence for the effectiveness of MICBT

Both MI and CBT have their own impressive evidence bases, so what might be the rationale for their integration? In the earlier (and indeed the later) chapters, we outline our thoughts about the contribution that MI might make to CBT practice, in terms of specifically considering and addressing motivational factors, but what does the literature say? From an evidence-informed perspective, this chapter looks at some of the potential benefits of integrating MI and CBT based on empirical findings.

Evidence for the impact of MICBT

There is limited scope within this chapter to explore the full and expanding body of literature looking at the effectiveness of MICBT, but this section will give a flavour or some of the research already completed, as well as key findings.

One significant study was a systematic literature review conducted by Marker and Norton (2018), which examined the impact of using MI as a prelude to CBT (MI+CBT) compared to CBT alone for anxiety disorders, across 12 studies. Across the studies, MI+CBT significantly outperformed CBT in terms of reducing clients' anxiety symptoms, although notably drop-out rates were not affected. From the findings, Marker and Norton (2018) proposed that even a single session of MI prior to the CBT could improve client outcomes.

Riper et al. (2014) described a meta-analysis of studies combining MI and CBT for supporting clients with 'alcohol use disorder' and major depression. Across the 12 identified studies, the authors found a small, but clinically significant effect of using MICBT, compared to treatment as usual. Barrett, Begg, O'Halloran and Kingsley (2018) reported similar findings from their meta-analysis of MICBT's effectiveness in promoting physical activity among overweight and obese adults.

Jones et al. (2011) investigated integrated CBT and MI for clients with bipolar disorder and comorbid substance use. MI was used, until a formulation was agreed and a commitment to change achieved, after which CBT strategies were employed. Notably MI strategies were resumed when motivational issues arose. The study was small-scale and described the use of integrated MICBT within five case studies. Typically, the participants did not describe their substance use as a primary concern, but in all but one case self-reported use decreased over the course of the therapy and at six-month follow-up. The descriptive case studies exemplified the complexity of the clients' lives and the way in which aspects of MI and CBT complimented each other within the therapeutic approach.

Advantages of MICBT as an integrated approach

One study mentioned in Marker and Norton's (2018) review offered clients a single 50-minute session of MI prior to a 12-week group CBT intervention for anxiety (Barrera, Smith & Norton, 2016). The authors found that those who received MI were significantly more likely to start the programme. They also attended more sessions and had higher completion rates, although differences here were not statistically significant. However, it seemed as if the benefits only lasted until around the fifth session of CBT, leading Marker and Norton (2018) to call for greater integration of the two approaches, rather than using MI as just an 'add-on'.

One advantage of using MI and CBT in a more integrated way might be cost efficiency. Barrera et al. (2016) suggested that providing multiple sessions of MI as a prelude to CBT might prove to be a burden on clinical settings with already stretched resources. Another reason is that where client feedback has been sought about using MI before CBT, this has suggested that adding MI improves the therapeutic relationship and can lead to better outcomes. This is explored in more depth in Chapter 13.

Barrett et al. (2018) proposed that integrating the two approaches might overcome documented shortcomings with both MI and CBT and offer a collaborative and directive approach. The authors did however suggest that greater attention needed to be paid to MICBT fidelity and this will be discussed further in Chapter 28.

Therapist views about MI and CBT integration

Although not directly related to effectiveness in terms of client outcomes, an interesting study by Iarussi and Osborn (2014) investigated the experience of six therapists who used MI and CBT in combination across different areas of practice. Analysis of interviews with the therapists revealed that they were able to use both approaches together, but notably only used CBT when they believed that the client was ready for change, as was the pattern in Jones et al.'s (2011) study. Given that Miller and Rollnick (2013) reported that there is some evidence that MI alone might deter progress for clients who are at the 'action' stage of change (see Chapter 7 on the transtheoretical model and Chapter 30 on ethical practice), within an integrated approach, it might be appropriate to consider MI as the lead therapy up to the point at which the client is ready for change, and CBT thereafter. Revisiting MI where motivational issues then present (Jones et al., 2011) is also advocated.

Summary

1. Research evidence suggests that using MI as a prelude to CBT can improve client engagement and outcomes.

2. Using a more integrated approach might help prolong the benefits of the initial MI interactions and provide a more cost-effective service.
3. Client readiness for change might be the point at which the therapist switches from MI to CBT as the main modality.

References

Barrera, T. L., Smith, A. H., & Norton, P. J. (2016). Motivational interviewing as an adjunct to cognitive behavioral therapy for anxiety. *Journal of Clinical Psychology*, *72*(1), 5–14. doi:10.1002/jclp.22239

Barrett, S., Begg, S., O'Halloran, P., & Kingsley, M. (2018). Integrated motivational interviewing and cognitive behaviour therapy for lifestyle mediators of overweight and obesity in community-dwelling adults: A systematic review and meta-analyses. *BMC Public Health*, *18*(1160), 1–10. doi:10.1186/s12889-018-6062-9

Iarussi, M. M., & Osborn, C. J. (2014). Counselors' experiences using motivational interviewing and cognitive behavior therapy. *Journal of Counselor Leadership and Advocacy*, *1*(1), 28–43. doi:10.1080/2326716X.2014.886979

Jones, S. H., Barrowclough, C., Allott, R., Day, C., Earnshaw, P., & Wilson, I. (2011). Integrated motivational interviewing and cognitive-behavioural therapy for bipolar disorder with comorbid substance use. *Clinical Psychology and Psychotherapy*, *18*(5), 426–437. doi:10.1002/cpp.783

Marker, I., & Norton, P. J. (2018). The efficacy of incorporating motivational interviewing to cognitive behavior therapy for anxiety disorders: A review and meta-analysis. *Clinical Psychology Review*, *62*(April), 1–10. doi:10.1016/j.cpr.2018.04.004

Miller, W. R., & Rollnick, S. (2013). *Motivational interviewing, third edition: Helping people change*. New York: Guilford Press.

Riper, H., Andersson, G., Hunter, S. B., de Wit, J., Berking, M., & Cuijpers, P. (2014). Treatment of comorbid alcohol use disorders and depression with cognitive-behavioural therapy and motivational interviewing: A meta-analysis. *Addiction*, *109*(3), 394–406. doi:10.1111/add.12441

11

Mechanisms for change

While there is growing evidence for the effectiveness of MICBT, there has been recent interest into why MI works and into the mechanisms which promote positive outcomes for clients. In this chapter, we will consider the different variables which potentially make therapy more effective and consider how these could influence MICBT practice.

Mechanisms for change within MI

Apodaca and Longabaugh (2009) identified that while there was growing evidence for the effectiveness of MI across clinical settings, there was little research about the mechanisms for change within therapy, or the 'active ingredients' which were most useful to clients. Initially, the authors identified four potentially important dimensions: MI spirit (see Chapter 8), MI-consistent behaviours, MI-inconsistent behaviours and specific techniques. Later Copeland et al. (2015) undertook a systematic literature review of mechanisms of change within MI in health behaviours and defined a number of dimensions of client and therapist behaviours (see Table 11.1). They also identified other client and therapist mediators, specifically: the therapeutic alliance, commitment strength and perceived behavioural control. Copeland et al. (2015) proposed that through understanding these facilitative mechanisms, MI practice could be enhanced and developed.

Copeland et al. (2015) found the strongest evidence for MI spirit and motivation being the most promising mechanisms within MI. Although there are limitations to the systematic literature, this suggests that two useful starting points for CBT

Table 11.1 MI mechanisms definitions (adapted from Copeland et al., 2015)

Therapist behaviours

Empathy	Seeing the world through the client's eyes and showing that you understand them from their perspective (see Chapter 4)
MI spirit	Based on key elements of acceptance, collaboration, compassion and evocation (see Chapter 8)
Reflections	To repeat or rephrase what the client has said allowing deeper meaning to the communication (see Chapter 23)
Open questions	Open-ended questions facilitate a client's response to questions from his or her own perspective and from the area(s) that are deemed important or relevant (see Chapter 21)
MI consistent	Defined as incorporating the following behaviours: advise with permission; affirm; emphasise control; open question; simple reflection; complex reflection; reframe; and support
MI inconsistent	Defined as incorporating the following behaviours: advise without permission; confront; direct; raise concern without permission and warn. If MI is delivered well there should be a low occurrence of MI-inconsistent behaviours and these should be inversely related to outcome.

Client behaviours

Change talk	Defined as statements by the client revealing consideration of, motivation for or commitment to change. There are different categories of change and sustain talk: ability, desire, reason, need, commitment, activation and taking steps (see Chapter 19).
Sustain talk	Statements made by the client in favour of the status quo (see Chapter 19).

(Continued)

Client behaviours

Self-efficacy	People's beliefs about their capabilities to change aspects of their lives. Self-efficacy includes both having the skills and the confidence (see Chapter 9).
Self-monitoring	Monitoring one's behaviour (e.g. via charts, diaries or self-weighing)
Stage of change	Behaviour involves stages of change: from precontemplation through to maintenance and determination. The change process unfolds over time, with progress through the stages, although frequently not in a linear manner (see Chapter 6)
Motivation	The process that initiates, guides and maintains goal-oriented behaviours (see Chapters 3 and 7)
Planning	Ideas of how the client can change their behaviour: these may include how, when and where (see Chapter 20).
Therapeutic alliance	The relationship between the client and the therapist (see Chapter 4).
Commitment strength	How committed an individual is to changing their behaviour
Perceived behavioural control	Defined as a person's perceptions of their ability to perform a certain behaviour

practitioners wishing to maximise outcomes might be an understanding of motivational theory and practising the MI spirit. Miller and Moyers (2006) recommended that learning the MI spirit should be the first step in training (see Chapter 28).

There were mixed findings for other mechanisms, including empathy, open questions, reflections and MI-consistent behaviour. Interestingly, evidence was weak for self-efficacy, which is interesting given its importance as a concept within MI, although Copeland et al. (2015) noted that the quality of the self-efficacy measures used was poor, which may have affected findings.

One area not considered specifically elsewhere in this book was self-monitoring, which was influential albeit with mixed results. Other areas which have received less attention – commitment strength and perceived behavioural control – did not appear to have significant impact. For this reason, this chapter will briefly take a closer look at self-monitoring, before finally considering the role of other mechanisms in MICBT practice.

Self-monitoring

Miller and Rollnick (2013) described self-monitoring as a way of strengthening commitment, which can be helpful to clients in terms of helping them remember their goal and to track progress. Suggested forms of self-monitoring include a diary, note cards, counting systems and regular checks (e.g. using the bathroom scales). Self-monitoring is commonplace in CBT through, for example, thought records and homework tasks, which are then reviewed in therapy. Roth and Pilling (2007) proposed that self-monitoring allows the client to "act as their own therapist" (p. 10), making the approach highly consistent with MI aspirations of promoting autonomy.

Why is understanding mechanisms important?

Understanding mechanisms for change helps us identify potentially important features within the intervention itself and how these relate to outcomes. Atkinson and Snape (2018) used Copeland et al.'s (2015) mechanisms as a way of mapping the body of literature on school-based MI practice, noticing that some of the mechanisms listed appeared to be more or less important with children and young people. Notably Copeland et al.'s (2015) review was based in healthcare settings, and therapists may find that other potentially 'active ingredients' are more relevant to clients in different contexts.

Finally, the reason why Table 11.1 is potentially useful in CBT is because the majority of these mediating factors are directly related to motivation. As mentioned previously, this is an area sometimes overlooked in CBT practice, and having greater awareness of these elements is potentially useful to therapists, both in terms of planning interventions and promoting positive outcomes.

Romano and Peters (2016) explored MI mechanisms, with reference to Miller and Rose's (2009) proposal of relational and technical MI components (see Chapter 12). They found that both the therapeutic style of MI and the specific techniques used in MI can directly affect client outcomes or facilitate client expression of change talk, which in turn is related to client outcomes. Also, they observed that trained MI clinicians using MI-consistent skills within a MI spirit are likely to see increased expression of change talk and reduced resistance within MI therapy. The reduction of resistance might be conceptualised as reducing sustain talk and could be seen as a possible mechanism of change.

Summary

1. A number of mechanisms for change have been identified within MI practice. Those which seem to have the greatest impact are MI spirit and motivation.
2. Understanding MI mechanisms can be helpful for CBT therapists to consider within their practice, particularly as most relate to client motivation.

References

Apodaca, T. R., & Longabaugh, R. (2009). Mechanisms of change in motivational interviewing: A review and preliminary evaluation of the evidence. *Addiction, 104*(5), 705–715.

Atkinson, C., & Snape, L. (2018). Mechanisms for change within school-based motivational interviewing: A review of the literature.

In McNamara, E. (Ed) *Motivational interviewing with children and young people III: Education and community settings* (pp. 59–75). Ainsdale: Positive Behaviour Management.

Copeland, L., McNamara, R., Kelson, M., & Simpson, S. (2015). Mechanisms of change within motivational interviewing in relation to health behaviors outcomes: A systematic review. *Patient Education and Counseling*, *98*(4), 401–411. doi:10.1016/j.pec.2014.11.022

Miller, W. R., & Moyers, T. B. (2006). Eight stages in learning motivational interviewing. *journal of teaching in the addictions*, *5*(1), 3–17. doi:10.1300/J188v05n01

Miller, W. R., & Rollnick, S. (2013). *Motivational interviewing, third edition: Helping people change*. New York: Guilford Press.

Miller, W. R., & Rose, G. S. (2009). Toward a theory of motivational interviewing. *The American Psychologist*, *64*(6), 527–537. doi:10.1037/a0016830

Romano, M., & Peters, L. (2016). Understanding the process of motivational interviewing: A review of the relational and technical hypotheses. *Psychotherapy Research: Journal of the Society for Psychotherapy Research*, *26*(2), 220–240. doi:10.1080/10503307.2014.954154

Roth, A. D., & Pilling, S. (2007). *The competences required to deliver effective cognitive and behavioural therapy for people with depression and with anxiety disorders*. London: Department of Health.

12

Relational and technical components of MICBT

In 2009, Miller and Rose proposed a new theory of MI, based on the idea that it included two active components. Relational components of MI related to empathy and the spirit of MI, while the technical components focused on evoking change talk. This chapter will consider the applicability and usefulness of this conceptualisation within MICBT and also whether or not these dimensions could be represented more clearly for the practitioner within MI literature. The description of these components as specific (technical) and non-specific (relational) (Miller & Rose, 2009) will be explored and challenged, the argument being that specifying components of general, relational factors can be potentially beneficial within MICBT.

Relational components of MICBT

Miller and Rose (2009) highlighted the role of empathy in relational factors as well as Rogers's (1959) other core conditions of acceptance (unconditional positive regard) and congruence (see Chapter 5). Later Miller and Moyers (2017) defined the MI spirit component as being synonymous with relational factors, possibly after Csillik (2013) proposed that the relational skills of MI should be more clearly defined and operationalised and that more research should be undertaken on the link between relational factors in MI and treatment outcomes.

We feel that the idea of relational and technical factors in MI could be further developed and investigated. For example, considering the processes and skills of MI (Chapters 17–24), it is plausible that these could be considered in both categories. For example, it could be argued that the process of engaging (Chapter 17) is largely relational and about developing the therapeutic alliance while the protocol Gobat et al. (2018) developed for the focusing process (see Chapter 18) includes assessment of both relational and technical skills.

Driessen and Hollon (2011) argued that a strength of MI in enhancing CBT practice is its clear delineation of relational factors through the spirit. We also argue therefore, that the idea of non-specific or generic factors in therapy (Miller & Moyers, 2017; Rogers, 1959) is a misnomer. MI is very specific about the nature of the relationship it wishes to create between therapist and client, which may not be a feature of other therapeutic modalities, including CBT (Driessen & Hollon, 2011). Cooke (2014) concluded that therapeutic alliance is seen to account for most of the within-therapy variance in trials and is up to seven times more influential in promoting change than the treatment model itself, while Hiebert (2005) suggested that the therapeutic alliance is key in providing the motivation to do the work of counselling.

This may be salutary for practitioners of CBT who hide behind CBT's extensive evidence base, without considering key factors like the therapeutic alliance and their own skills in relationship building, even though research has suggested that these skills mediate positive outcomes. Because the quality of the therapeutic alliance is such a potentially important factor in treatment outcome, it is therefore important for MICBT proponents to consider both the technical *and* relational skills involved in therapy.

Technical components of MICBT

Miller and Rose (2009) proposed that technical factors in MI related to increasing in-session change talk and decreasing sustain talk – that in favour of maintaining the current behaviour. Besides proposing that technical factors involve paying attention to certain aspects of the client's language, help promote a favourable outcome and should be undertaken from an empathic perspective, Miller and Moyers (2017) offered little additional guidance about what these technical elements should entail. By contrast, the technical skills of CBT are defined meticulously. Within their competency map for using CBT for supporting clients with anxiety or depression, Roth and Pilling (2007) identified a whole host of specific techniques as well as problem-specific competencies (e.g. approaches to be used in the treatment of social phobia or post-traumatic stress disorder [PTSD]). It is possibly that this makes CBT easier to learn than MI, which research has shown takes considerable time and opportunity to develop proficiency (Hall, Staiger, Simpson, Best & Lubman, 2016). It also means that there is likely to be greater practice consistency with technical elements of CBT, as these are better defined. This might also account for the lack of practice consistency within MI (Frost et al., 2018) and might even be a factor in why MI appears to be less effective for clients who want to change their behaviour (Miller & Rollnick, 2013). This is another reason for using CBT and MI together, as evidence suggests CBT is more effective than MI once clients are ready for change.

Summary

1. Miller and Rose (2009) distinguished between relational and technical factors in therapy. Attention to both is important in maximising outcomes for clients.
2. MI offers a clearer protocol for relational factors, whereas CBT defines technical factors much more clearly. Therefore, in offering the most effective therapeutic approach, it seems logical to integrate MI and CBT.

References

Cooke, A. (Ed). (2014). *Understanding psychosis. Understanding psychosis and schizophrenia*. Leicester: British Psychological Society Division of Clinical Psychology. doi:10.4324/9781351025942

Csillik, A. S. (2013). Understanding motivational interviewing effectiveness: Contributions from Rogers' client-centered approach. *Humanistic Psychologist*, *41*(4), 350–363. doi:10.1080/08873267.2013.779906

Driessen, E., & Hollon, S. D. (2011). Motivational interviewing from a cognitive behavioral perspective. *Cognitive and Behavioral Practice*, *18*(1), 70–73. doi:10.1016/j.cbpra.2010.02.007

Frost, H., Campbell, P., Maxwell, M., Carroll, R. E. O., Dombrowski, U., Williams, B., … Pollock, A. (2018). Effectiveness of motivational interviewing on adult behaviour change in health and social care settings: A systematic review of reviews. *PLoS ONE*, *155*, 1–39.

Gobat, N., Copeland, L., Cannings-john, R., Robling, M., Carpenter, J., Cowley, L., … Sanders, J. (2018). "Focusing" in Motivational interviewing: Development of a training tool for practitioners. *European Journal for Person Centered Healthcare*, *6*(1), 37–49.

Hall, K., Staiger, P. K., Simpson, A., Best, D., & Lubman, D. I. (2016). After 30 years of dissemination, have we achieved sustained practice change in motivational interviewing? *Addiction*, *111*(7), 1144–1150. doi:10.1111/add.13014

Hiebert, B. (2005). *Creating a working alliance: Generic interpersonal skills and Concepts*. Calgary, AB: University of Calgary. Retrieved from http://drr.lib.athabascau.ca/files/psyc/405/bhiebert.pdf

Miller, W. R., & Moyers, T. B. (2017). Motivational interviewing and the clinical science of Carl Rogers. *Journal of Consulting and Clinical Psychology*, *85*(8), 757–766. doi:10.1037/ccp0000179

Miller, W. R., & Rollnick, S. (2013). *Motivational interviewing, third edition: Helping people change*. New York: Guilford Press.

Miller, W. R., & Rose, G. S. (2009). Toward a theory of motivational interviewing. *The American Psychologist*, *64*(6), 527–537. doi:10.1037/a0016830

Rogers, C. R. (1959). A theory of therapy, personality and interpersonal relationships as developed in the client-centred framework. In S. Koch (Ed.), *Psychology: The study of science (Vol. 3). Formulations of the person and the social context* (pp. 184–256). New York: McGraw-Hill.

Roth, A. D., & Pilling, S. (2007). *The competences required to deliver effective cognitive and behavioural therapy for people with depression and with anxiety disorders*. London: Department of Health.

13

Client perspectives

There is a growing evidence base identifying the components of MICBT which clients identify as being instrumentally helpful in promoting change. This chapter will examine emergent findings, considering how these might be beneficial in informing practice and in developing evidence-based integrative practice in MICBT. The chapter will also explore how client views might be captured and used to inform therapist development and to improve outcomes.

Client-reported benefits of using an integrated approach

In order to understand the potential benefits for clients from using an MICBT approach, it is useful to consider some of the research which has described client experiences of an MI-focused CBT intervention. Angus and Kagan (2009) explored the views of a client with generalised anxiety disorder about a four-week MI intervention which was provided as a precursor to a 14-week CBT intervention. The client reported that after the MI and prior to the CBT that the MI gave her the opportunity to speak openly and offered her strength and courage. Notably the MI helped make her some initial changes and enhanced her readiness for further change. Particularly valued were the therapist's empathic attunement, characterised by the MI spirit (see Chapter 8) and the creation of a safe space for sharing her concerns.

Kertes, Westra, Angus and Marcus (2011) compared the experience of ten clients who had received CBT for generalised anxiety, five of whom had received MI pretreatment. Clients who received the MI described the therapists as 'evocative guides' and felt that they played an active role within therapy, while those in the CBT-only group described the same therapists as directive and felt that they were more passive recipients of therapy. MI was perceived as allowing preparation for change; CBT as offering the tools for enabling change.

Jones, Latchford and Tober (2016) allowed clients who had received MI for problematic drinking to reflect on video recordings of their session and comment on important moments. The clients felt that the MI had emphasised their autonomy, helped them to feel listened to and elicited their own views. They also noted that confrontation was avoided, that the therapist offered a non-judgemental approach and that the relationship felt collaborative.

Client evaluation in MICBT

There has been published evaluation of clients' experience of CBT, including personal perceptions of formulation (Redhead, Johnstone, & Nightingale, 2015) and outcome and session ratings (Janse, De Jong, Van Dijk, Hutschemaekers, & Verbraak, 2017). In relation to MI, Madson and colleagues (cf. Madson, Villarosa, Schumacher, & Mohn, 2016) have undertaken significant work into finding ways to capture client views about the process. Specifically, they provided a validated self-report measure – the client evaluation of MI (CEMI) to help therapists understand the way in which MI was experienced by the client. The CEMI is based upon the spirit, principles and skills of MI (see Chapters 8, 9 and 21–24) and can offer the therapist feedback about the quality of therapist–client interactions, which can be used for development and within supervision.

Specifically, the CEMI asks for client feedback on 12 items rated on a Likert scale from 1 (not at all) to 4 (a great deal) to the question "During your most recent counselling session how much did your clinician [demonstrate each behaviour]?" The items are shown in Figure 13.1.

CEMI Items

1. *Examine your strengths*
2. Help you talk about changing your behaviour
3. *Make you talk about something you did not want to discuss**
4. Help you discuss your need to change your behaviour
5. Help you examine the pros and cons of changing your behaviour
6. *Argue with you to change your behaviour**
7. *Help you feel hopeful about changing your behaviour.*
8. Act as a partner in your behaviour change.
9. Help you recognise the need to change your behaviour
10. *Tell you what to do**
11. Help you feel confident in your ability to change your behaviour.
12. *Acts as an authority in your life**

Figure 13.1 Items on the CEMI rating scale (Madson et al., 2016)

Note: Items in normal type relate to technical factors, while items in italics address relationship factors. Asterisked items are reverse-scaled.

An advantage of the CEMI is that it gives the therapist immediate feedback on the extent to which they are following motivational principles and acting in an MI-adherent way. However, none of the items is MI-specific, and the scale could just as easily be used within CBT, or indeed any other form of counselling or therapy. The client's answers are likely to provide considerable insight into the extent to which they feel in control of the therapeutic process, to what extent they are affirmed, encouraged and listened to and whether they feel that the interaction feels like a partnership. This feedback can also help the therapist gain insight into the extent to which motivational factors are being addressed within MICBT.

Why is positive client evaluation important?

Madson et al. (2016) noted that client perceptions of counselling are often better predictors of treatment outcomes than therapist observations, and can improve outcomes when used routinely within monitoring, and enhance skill development in therapists.

We are not necessarily suggesting that client views always need to be formally evaluated or measured. However, it is feasible that CEMI items could be used in informal discussions, for therapist self-reflection, or within supervision to allow development and enhancement of practice and to provide client-centred therapy, which minimises the risk of drop-out and maximises client outcomes.

Summary

1. Evidence from client feedback suggests that using MI as a precursor to CBT enhances the therapeutic relationship, the client's sense of autonomy and partnership, and their readiness for change.
2. Assessing client perceptions of therapy, using the CEMI or other formal or informal measures can help promote therapist skills and lead to better outcomes for clients.

References

Angus, L. E., & Kagan, F. (2009). Therapist empathy and client anxiety reduction in motivational interviewing: "She carries with me, the experience." *Journal of Clinical Psychology in Session*, *65*(11), 1156–1167. doi:10.1002/jclp

Janse, P. D., De Jong, K., Van Dijk, M. K., Hutschemaekers, G. J. M., & Verbraak, M. J. P. M. (2017). Improving the efficiency of cognitive-behavioural therapy by using formal client feedback. *Psychotherapy Research*, *27*(5), 525–538. doi:10.1080/10503307.2016.11 52408

Jones, S. A., Latchford, G., & Tober, G. (2016). Client experiences of motivational interviewing: An interpersonal process recall study. *Psychology and Psychotherapy: Theory, Research and Practice*, *89*(1), 97–114. doi:10.1111/papt.12061

Kertes, A., Westra, H. A., Angus, L., & Marcus, M. (2011). The impact of motivational interviewing on client experiences of cognitive behavioral therapy for generalized anxiety disorder. *Cognitive and Behavioral Practice*, *18*(1), 55–69. doi:10.1016/j.cbpra.2009.06.005

Madson, M. B., Villarosa, M. C., Schumacher, J. A., & Mohn, R. S. (2016). Evaluating the validity of the client evaluation of motivational interviewing scale in a brief motivational intervention for college student drinkers. *Journal of Substance Abuse Treatment*, *65*, 51–57. doi:10.1016/j.jsat.2016.02.001

Redhead, S., Johnstone, L., & Nightingale, J. (2015). Clients' experiences of formulation in cognitive behaviour therapy. *Psychology and Psychotherapy: Theory, Research and Practice*, *88*(4), 453–467. doi:10.1111/papt.12054

14

Differences and similarities between MI and CBT

In the first section of the book, we have introduced motivational and MI theory and discussed its potential contribution to CBT theory and practice. This chapter will summarise similarities and differences between MI and CBT practice, and in doing so, describe how combining the approaches can be mutually beneficial. The chapter will first compare the theoretical emergence of both approaches, and then contrast CBT and MI practice. Differences in emphasis will be highlighted, before techniques from both approaches which can be incorporated into existing practice are suggested.

Development of theory

Neither CBT nor MI developed out of theory, and both initially derived from clinical practice, although arguably the origins of MI in particular are theoretically informed (see Chapter 4). Both approaches originate from different professional frameworks that were prevalent in the late 1970s and early 1980s. In terms of emergence within professional fields, key proponents of CBT, for example Aaron Beck and Albert Ellis, were psychoanalytic psychiatrists. By contrast the main protagonists of MI – William Miller and Stephen Rollnick – were clinical psychologists with behaviour therapy backgrounds.

CBT developed in part out of a reaction to psychodynamic practice, while MI is grounded in humanistic, client-centred therapy and includes some elements of behaviour therapy. Within MI limited attention is paid to cognitive processes, although cognitive change is both a mechanism and a goal. MI, defined as a "collaborative, goal-orientated style of communication" (Miller & Rollnick, 2013, p. 29), places more emphasis on creating a safe space where people are free to explore thoughts feelings and behaviours in relation to a specific goal. By contrast, CBT's main focus is on the interrelationship between thoughts, feelings and behaviour.

Both MI and CBT can be said to be person-centred, but each might dispute how genuinely this is the case. For example, MI is more directional than Rogerian counselling (see Chapter 5) in that there is often a specific reason why the therapist would be looking to help the client reduce their ambivalence (e.g. improved adherence to medical treatment, or less risk of harm through alcohol use). CBT uses a Socratic approach to guide individuals towards a cognitive or behavioural discovery. MI places emphasis not only on building motivation through exploration but also on the differential reinforcement of talk about change (see Chapter 20). The underlying philosophy or spirit of MI is specified (see Chapter 8) and also observable at the level of skill in practice (see Chapter 28). CBT pays less specific attention to this relational element and arguably pays insufficient to addressing motivation in those who are ambivalent, both in terms of identifying it as an issue and offering strategies for building client motivation. However, it could be contended that the acquisition of new skills and knowledge offered through CBT may be seen as motivating in itself.

In their paper, "Ten Things that Motivational Interviewing Is Not", Miller and Rollnick (2009) specified (at number 6) that "MI is not a form of cognitive-behaviour therapy" (p. 134). Specific reasons provided included:

- Unlike MI, CBT generally involves providing clients with something they are presumed to lack (e.g. coping skills, psychoeducation).
- MI does not seek to correct erroneous beliefs.

- The therapist takes the position of companion, rather than expert.
- The conceptual basis of MI is humanistic, rather than behavioural.

Miller (2017) argued that at some levels CBT and MI seem completely opposite, with CBT practised from a directive, expert model focussed on installing what the client lacks, while MI is about building on the client's existing motivation, wisdom and ideas. However, he also recognised that they are "not only compatible, but complementary" (p. vii).

Practice

MI has established itself as an approach that is effective at building motivation for change and has begun to develop theory as to why it is an effective behaviour change intervention (de Almeida Neto, 2017; Miller & Rose, 2009). MI emphasises that the client is the expert on themselves, while CBT is more educational and generally assumes that expert information and formulation will be helpful. MI promotes information giving with the client's permission but emphasises eliciting what the client knows already.

MI and CBT have both been can be seen to be trans-diagnostic and can be applied with a range of presenting behaviours. MI was originally developed from Miller's (1983) work with problem drinkers, but has since become prominent across a whole range of health, educational, social care and forensic behaviours. However, while both approaches are trying help people understand the origins of their problematic behaviours, CBT offers diagnostically specific models (e.g. for obsessive-compulsive disorder [OCD]) and formulations to discuss the impact of current thoughts, feelings and behaviours. Conversely, MI is not diagnostic or model-specific and instead focuses on the person and their strengths and capabilities. Individualised formulation has developed in CBT over a number of years and may have led to some practice becoming more person-centred. Labelling has been avoided in MI from its outset.

Both CBT and MI are individualised therapies although both have developed group interventions and CBT has developed adaptations for working with families.

Differences in emphasis

While it is not possible to describe all of the similarities and differences in this chapter alone, many of them are described at other points in the book. Table 14.1 details some of the main differences in emphasis between CBT and MI, in some cases signposting the reader to other chapters for further information.

As well as the differences, we have also given consideration to the strengths of both approaches. In using a MICBT approach, therapists whose main modality is either CBT or MI may wish to draw on some of the components of the other approach to strengthen their practice. For this purpose, possible key concepts to integrate are included in Table 14.2.

Table 14.1 Summary of the differences in emphasis between CBT and MI

Cognitive behavioural therapy	Motivational interviewing
Problem-focussed	Strengths-focussed
Formulation-led	Target behaviour-led
Schema core beliefs	Values and goals
Expert-led	Expert trap (Miller & Rollnick, 2013); avoids the righting reflex (see Chapter 16)
How to change	Why change?
Thoughts-feelings-behaviour	Values-goals, dissonance-behaviour (see Chapters 9 and 25)
Change as a function of the individual	Change as a function of the relationship (see Chapter 7)

Table 14.2 What to integrate from CBT and MI

What to integrate from CBT	*What to integrate from MI*
Agenda	Listening for and responding to readiness to change (see Chapter 19)
Skills training	Identifying core values (see Chapter 25)
Formulation	Working with ambivalence
Identifying beliefs	Evocation (see Chapter 19)
Explicit roles in therapy	Autonomy – client as agent of change *not* the therapy (see Chapters 4 and 8)
Problem solving	Supporting self-efficacy (see Chapter 9)
Behavioural experiments	Reflective listening (see Chapter 21)
Emphasis on self-monitoring	Affirmation (see Chapter 22)

Summary

1. While there are many similarities between CBT and MI, there are a considerable number of differences, including theoretical origins and the perceived role of the therapist.
2. CBT and MI can complement each other. Introduction of MI approaches into CBT, and vice-versa can potentially help develop practice and improve client outcomes.

References

de Almeida Neto, A. C. (2017). Understanding motivational interviewing: An evolutionary perspective. *Evolutionary Psychological Science*, *3*, 379–389. doi:10.1007/s40806-017-0096-6

Miller, W. R. (1983). Motivational interviewing with problem drinkers. *Behavioural Psychotherapy*, *11*(2), 147–172. doi:10.1017/S0141347300006583

Miller, W. R. (2017). Foreword. In S. Naar & S. A. Safren (Eds.), *Motivational interviewing and CBT* (pp. vii–x). New York: Guilford.

Miller, W. R., & Rollnick, S. (2009). Ten things that motivational interviewing is not. *Behavioural and Cognitive Psychotherapy*, *37*, 129–140. doi:10.1017/S1352465809005128

Miller, W. R., & Rollnick, S. (2013). *Motivational interviewing, third edition: Helping people change*. New York: Guilford Press.

Miller, W. R., & Rose, G. S. (2009). Toward a theory of motivational interviewing. *The American Psychologist*, *64*(6), 527–537. doi:10.1037/a0016830

15

MI, CBT and other approaches

CBT has developed into a variety of different forms including what are now called third-wave CBTs including acceptance and commitment therapy (ACT), cognitive behaviour therapy for psychosis (CBT(p)), cognitive therapy (CT), compassion focussed therapy (CFT), dialectical behaviour therapy (DBT), meta cognitive therapy (MCT) and mindfulness-based cognitive behaviour therapy (MBCBT). Miller and Moyers (2017) noted that innovations tend to be adopted when they are compatible with other practices and that MI can be a complementary method which can be used alongside other approaches. Miller and Moyers (2006) noted that MI training should build up to switching between MI and other counselling modalities.

Unfortunately, there is not space within this chapter to consider integration of all of the third-wave CBT approaches, and MI. For this reason, attention will be paid to two specific approaches – ACT and CFT – which have already been the focus of MI integration within the literature. The chapter will consider advantages and issues of integrating the approaches, before briefly considering general issues with integrating MI with CBT and CBT-based approaches.

ACT and MI

Harris (2019) noted that ACT derived from the work of Stephen Hayes in the late 1980s and offers a therapeutic approach in which action is guided by the client's core values and aspirations (see also Chapter 25) as well as mindful action. Bricker and

Tollison (2011) noted that ACT and MI share a number of common elements including the following:

- Enhancing commitment for behavioural change
- Using the client's values and aspirations to promote commitment
- Working within the medium of the client's language
- Expressing empathy
- Developing an awareness of the discrepancy between the current behaviour and important goals or values
- Avoiding struggling with resistance.

However, unlike MI, ACT offers psychoeducation in teaching specific skills to promote acceptance of difficult thoughts, feelings and sensations. ACT also seeks more actively to change patterns of language which inhibit change, whereas MI is more focussed on harnessing and amplifying change talk. In terms of developing a therapeutic relationship, ACT places more emphasis on shared suffering and self-disclosure than MI; and while MI focuses on the OARS skills within communication (see Chapters 21–24), ACT tends to use metaphor and experiential activities to allow clients to experience the ACT process.

Bricker and Tollison (2011) described ways in which ACT and MI could be mutually complementary. These included:

- Encouraging therapists working within ACT to roll with resistance (see Chapter 9)
- Using OARS skills within ACT (see Chapters 21–24)
- Making greater use of metaphor within MI
- Clinical use of the values card sort (see Chapter 25) within ACT.

CFT and MI

Developed by Paul Gilbert (cf. Gilbert, 2010), CFT is developed on the premise of human evolutionary responses to three basic motivational systems: the threat/self-protect system, the drive/reward system and the affiliative/soothing system. Steindl, Kirby and Tellegan (2018) highlighted how humans trapped within the threat and drive systems can experience emotions such as shame or self-criticism, and that therefore activities which facilitate compassion via the soothing system can have therapeutic benefits.

Steindl et al. (2018) noted that CFT incorporates a range of exercises to develop self-compassion, including psychoeducation, body posture and mindfulness, imagery, breathing and behavioural rehearsal (such as compassionate letter writing or method acting). However, client autonomy is promoted in allowing the client to engage in relevant activities meaningfully, rather than seeing them as prescriptive. Both client autonomy and compassion are central to the spirit of MI (see Chapter 8).

In relation to change talk, Steindl et al. (2018) noted that MI has resonance with CFT, which tries to draw upon the client's wisdom in knowing which CFT-based exercises to engage with meaningfully. This also fits with Miller and Rollnick's (2013) advocacy of clients being the experts in themselves. Steindl et al. (2018) proposed that MI could support CFT in the following ways (p. 273):

1. Session attendance
2. Completion of self-practice for homework
3. Engaging with aspects of suffering that the client would rather avoid
4. Taking steps towards incorporating compassionate or self-compassionate actions into daily life.

Steindl et al. (2018) also suggested that notions of change and sustain talk (see Chapter 19) can be useful in allowing clients to explore facilitators of compassion, including benefits, links with values, confidence and coping strategies along with barriers, including fears and blocks to engaging with the activities listed above. Miller and Rollnick's (2013) notions of exploring motivation and confidence to change can also be used, alongside these conversations (see Chapter 19).

While MI can offer an opportunity to promote motivation and commitment for engagement with CFT practices, the argument can also be made that CFT offers practical, tangible and technical interventions which can promote change as well as emotional health and well-being. CFT exercises could provide the client with a range of potentially meaningful avenues for self-exploration and compassion-based living, at the point where they are ready to change their behaviour or lifestyle. As with CBT, CFT can potentially offer greater directionality and focus for clients who are preparing for change, or actively trying to change behaviour.

Summary

1. Comparisons made here between ACT and CFT and MI offer templates for how other therapeutic approaches, CBT-derived or otherwise, could be combined with MI to acknowledge motivation as a key factor, develop the therapeutic relationship, promote change talk and increase client autonomy.
2. With the focus of MI being on effective and person-centred communication, attention could be given to its potential contribution to other counselling domains and to how the skills of MI and other modalities could potentially strengthen the therapeutic offer, develop therapist skills and promote better outcomes for clients.

References

Bricker, J., & Tollison, S. (2011). Comparison of motivational interviewing with acceptance and commitment therapy: A conceptual and clinical review. *Behavioural and Cognitive Psychotherapy, 39*(5), 541–559. doi:10.1017/S1352465810000901

Gilbert, P. (2010). *The compassionate mind: A new approach to life's challenges*. London: Constable.

Harris, R. (2019). *ACT made simple: An easy-to-read primer on acceptance and commitment therapy*. Oakland, CA: New Harbinger Books.

Miller, W. R., & Moyers, T. B. (2006). Eight stages in learning motivational interviewing. *Journal of Teaching in the Addictions, 5*(1), 3–17. doi:10.1300/J188v05n01

Miller, W. R., & Moyers, T. B. (2017). Motivational interviewing and the clinical science of Carl Rogers. *Journal of Consulting and Clinical Psychology, 85*(8), 757–766. doi:10.1037/ccp0000179

Miller, W. R., & Rollnick, S. (2013). *Motivational interviewing, third edition: Helping people change*. New York: Guilford Press.

Steindl, S. R., Kirby, J. N., & Tellegan, C. (2018). Motivational interviewing in compassion-based interventions: Theory and practical applications. *Clinical Psychologist, 22*(3), 265–279. doi:10.1111/cp.12146

Part II

THE DISTINCTIVE PRACTICAL FEATURES OF MICBT

16

Avoiding the righting reflex

We now move on to the chapters describing practice in MICBT. Subsequently, we will look at the processes and skills of MI, frameworks and approaches for practice, systemic issues and ethics. We will start with an idea at the very heart of practical MI – the righting reflex.

MI is specific about the role of autonomy and self-direction in client change. Contrary to this is the righting reflex, which relates to the notion of the practitioner wanting to help the client and essentially trying to direct, persuade or coerce them into change. Within the context of nursing, Levensky, Forcehimes, O'Donohue and Beitz (2007) described the righting reflex as "the natural tendency to try to fix a patient's problems by imposing solutions on the patient" (p. 53). This chapter will consider reasons to avoid the righting reflex, offer strategies for avoiding it and describe its relevance to MICBT practice.

Reasons to avoid the righting reflex

Miller and Rollnick (2013) recognised the motives behind the righting reflex as wanting the best outcomes for the client. They acknowledged that some therapists hold the belief that if you ask the right questions, provide the proper information or engage in the appropriate arguments that the client will be convinced of, or persuaded into, change.

The reasons for avoiding the righting reflex lie in the notion of ambivalence, and Miller and Rollnick's (2013) metaphoric notion of a "committee" in your head is helpful here (see Chapter 2). The more strongly the therapist argues for change, the more strongly the elements of the committee seeking to sustain the behaviour become activated. Miller and Rollnick (2002) proposed that the inclination towards the righting reflex may be particularly strong where the therapist concludes that the client is "in denial" or "resisting" (p. 21), in which case, the therapist can intensify their argument, potentially leading the client to withdraw or avoid contact.

Miller and Rollnick (2002) observed that as well as arguing for change, the righting reflex led to a tendency to provide possible solutions for the client's perceived problem. What they noted was that clients tended to reject suggestions ("yes, but", "I've already tried…"), causing more frustration for both therapist and client and potentially jeopardising the therapeutic alliance. Rollnick, Kaplan and Rutschman (2016) proposed that using the righting reflex could reduce client problem solving, affect engagement and provide solutions with a narrow focus, which might not be relevant to the client.

Rollnick et al. (2016) talked about "taming" the righting reflex when suggesting MI as an approach for teachers working in schools. They described it as a less conscious, almost automatic response to a problem a client might be struggling with, both in terms of identifying the problem and telling the individual why and how to change.

How to avoid the righting reflex

In relation to offering any sort of support for behaviour change, this will depend on the client's readiness for change. In the following chapters, we will explore the four processes of MI – engaging, focusing, evoking and planning – which describe a hierarchical approach to working constructively with the client. We will also explore the core skills of MI – open questions, affirmations, reflections and summaries (OARS), which aim to foster motivation, autonomy and confidence in the client. In Chapter 26, we will consider, when and where appropriate, how to provide information to the client in an MI-adherent way, which avoids the righting reflex.

When there is an indication of a desire to change, a number of suggestions provided by Rollnick, Heather and Bell (1992) within their Menu of Strategies, under the item "helping with decision-making" (p. 33) are useful alternatives to the righting reflex. This approach allows the client to explore whether to change their behaviour or stay the same, while ensuring that therapist does not take over as "expert problem-solver" (p. 33). These eight key guidelines, contracted appropriately with the client (see Chapter 26), are broadly as follows:

- Do not rush clients into decision-making.
- Present different options for the future rather than a single course of action.
- Describe what other clients have done in a similar situation.
- In accordance with collaboration and the notion of a partnership between two experts (see Chapter 8), emphasise to the client that they will be the best judge of what is right for them.
- Provide any information in a neutral and non-personal manner.
- Ensure it is recognised that if a decision to change is not reached, this does not mean that the consultation has been unsuccessful.
- Resolutions to change often break down. It is important for clients to understand this, and to create a culture of acceptance so that the client will not avoid contact in the future. This is important in the event of relapse (see Chapter 7) to allow the client to quickly get back on track, should they wish to.
- Commitment to change is likely to fluctuate. Expect this to happen and empathise with the client's predicament.

The righting reflex and CBT practice

Driessen and Hollon (2011) acknowledged that it is neither the role of the cognitive behavioural therapist to tell clients what to believe, nor to tell the client what to do. While acknowledging that neither would be a feature of CBT the authors recognised that many aspects of MI provide a useful reminder to therapists about client-centred practice. We believe that noticing and adjusting practice to avoid the righting reflex is a helpful tenet for MICBT practice.

Summary

1. The righting reflex refers to the human instinct to try and make things right for the client.
2. The righting reflex is problematic, as it is likely to encourage ambivalent clients to become defensive and decrease feelings of autonomy and confidence.
3. Using the spirit and skills of MI skills within MICBT practice can help the therapist become vigilant for the righting reflex and create a therapeutic relationship in which responsibility for change lies with the client.

References

Driessen, E., & Hollon, S. D. (2011). Motivational interviewing from a cognitive behavioral perspective. *Cognitive and Behavioral Practice, 18*(1), 70–73. doi:10.1016/j.cbpra.2010.02.007

Levensky, E. R., Forcehimes, A., O'Donohue, W. T., & Beitz, K. (2007). Motivational interviewing: An evidence-based approach to counselling. *American Journal of Nursing, 107*(10), 50–58.

Miller, W. R., & Rollnick, S. (2002). *Motivational interviewing, second edition: Preparing people for change*. New York: Guilford Press.

Miller, W. R., & Rollnick, S. (2013). *Motivational interviewing, third edition: Helping people change*. New York: Guilford Press.

Rollnick, S., Heather, N., & Bell, A. (1992). Negotiating behaviour change in medical settings: The development of brief motivational interviewing. *Journal of Mental Health, 1*, 25–37. doi:10.3109/09638239209034509

Rollnick, S., Kaplan, S., & Rutschman, R. (2016). *Motivational interviewing in schools*. New York: Guilford Press.

17

MI processes – 1. Engaging

Miller and Rollnick (2013) defined four processes of MI shown in Figure 17.1, which are essentially hierarchical and should be undertaken in order (Frey, Sims, & Alvarez, 2013). The next four chapters will consider using the processes from a MICBT perspective, starting with the underpinning process of 'engaging'.

Engaging is an important feature of both MI and CBT. Roth and Pilling (2007, p. 17) defined engaging with the client as a core generic competency of CBT. Miller and Rollnick (2013) proposed engaging as the process by which both counsellor and client establish a helpful connection and working relationship – a "prerequisite for everything that follows" (p. 27). Sometimes described as rapport (e.g. Griffin & Tyrrell, 2003), engaging links closely to the notion of a therapeutic alliance. At a very basic level, Miller and Rollnick (2013) observed that engagement is

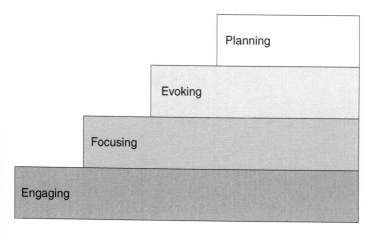

Figure 17.1 MI processes (Miller & Rollnick, 2013)

more likely to lead to the client returning, and that logically, if this is not achieved then further work is not possible.

Dorsey et al. (2014), who supplemented their trauma-focused CBT intervention for children and young people in foster care and their foster parents with engagement strategies, proposed that engagement interventions increase motivation to actively participate in treatment. As MI addresses engagement specifically, consideration of effective factors can potentially support CBT efficacy and improve client outcomes. Some key principles of engaging, defined by Miller and Rollnick (2013), are considered in the sections below.

Facilitating engagement and avoiding disengagement

Miller and Rollnick (2013) first identified factors that can both support and inhibit engagement. Specifically, they highlighted a number of "traps" that can jeopardise the therapeutic relationship in its early stages. These include:

- An over-reliance on assessment, for example the therapist asking questions and the client answering
- The therapist adopting the role of expert
- Trying to focus on key issues before a working relationship has been developed (focusing before engaging)
- Focusing on establishing a diagnosis or looking at whose fault the problem is.

All of these issues are worthy of consideration by CBT therapists, allowing both practice reflection or supervision foci.

Effective listening

While listening will be covered more comprehensively in other chapters, including those which address OARS skills, it is important to recognise the role of listening in engaging. In his book

Listening Well, Miller (2018) proposed that listening involves a skill set that goes beyond just keeping quiet, to actually try and perceive the meaning behind the underlying words and in doing so achieve accurate empathy. Conversely, Miller and Rollnick (2013) identified a number of "roadblocks" (p. 49) which inhibit client self-exploration and interfere with the therapist listening effectively. Often these relate to the righting reflex (see Chapter 16) and are typified by the therapist trying to take control of the interaction, rather than seeing the client as a partner. Instead, effective listening and careful reflection can help develop understanding of the client's situation, enhancing rapport and engagement.

Using OARS skills and exploring values and goals

The central skills of OARS – open questions, affirmations, reflections and summaries – are defined by Miller and Rollnick (2012) as core to communication and foundational to the four MI processes shown in Figure 17.1. Paying careful attention to these skills can be useful to CBT practitioners attempting to engage clients, particularly those who may not necessarily be ready to think about behavioural change (see Chapter 7). OARS skills will be explored in detail in Chapters 21–24.

Finally, Miller and Rollnick (2013) stressed that an important feature of engagement is understanding the client's internal frame of reference. This means it is important at the outset to explain their values, goals, strengths and aspirations. Failing to appreciate the world view of the client makes it difficult to support them in finding a way forward which is meaningful, achievable and sustainable for them.

Practising skills associated with reflection

Atkinson and Woods (2018) offered a checklist for practitioner reflection, for skills associated with the process of engaging, based on principles suggested by Miller and Rollnick (2012)

Engaging	Check □	Evidence
• The client understands my role and is clear about the reasons why we are working together.	□	
• I have explained boundaries of confidentiality to the client.	□	
• I have spent time learning about the client's achievements, strengths and preferences.	□	
• I am able to empathise with the client's predicament.	□	
• I have explored with the client their values and aspirations.	□	
• I have created time and space for the client to explain their perspective.	□	
• I have listened carefully to the client's perspective and try to reflect back how they are feeling.	□	

Figure 17.2 Protocol for practitioner reflection on the engagement process within MICBT

and Rollnick, Kaplan and Rutschman (2016). This is shown in Figure 17.2. It is envisaged that reflecting on these elements of MI engagement can enhance both effective engagement and the therapeutic alliance, within MICBT practice.

Summary

1. Engaging is the first of the four hierarchical processes of MI. It is also central to competence in CBT.
2. Engagement is enabled by partnership, effective listening, accurate empathy and appreciating the client's values and goals. It is inhibited by the therapist adopting the role of expert, or the righting reflex.

References

Atkinson, C., & Woods, K. (2018). Integrity in the delivery of school-based motivational interviewing: protocols for practitioners. In McNamara, E. (Ed.), *Motivational interviewing with children and young people III: Education and community settings* (pp. 76–92). Ainsdale: Positive Behaviour Management.

Dorsey, S., Pullmann, M. D., Berliner, L., Koschmann, E., McKay, M., & Deblinger, E. (2014). Engaging foster parents in treatment: A randomized trial of supplementing trauma-focused cognitive behavioral therapy with evidence-based engagement strategies. *Child Abuse and Neglect, 38*(9), 1508–1520. doi:10.1016/j.chiabu.2014.03.020

Frey, A. J., Sims, K., & Alvarez, M. E. (2013). The promise of motivational interviewing for securing a niche in the RtI movement. *Children & Schools, 35*(2), 67–70. doi:10.1093/cs/cdt004

Griffin, J., & Tyrrell, I. (2003). *Human givens: The new approach to emotional health and clear thinking*. Chalvington: HG Publishing.

Miller, W. R. (2018). *Listening well: The art of empathic understanding*. Eugene: Oregon: WIPF & Stock.

Miller, W. R., & Rollnick, S. (2013). *Motivational interviewing, third edition: Helping people change*. New York: Guilford Press.

Rollnick, S., Kaplan, S., & Rutschman, R. (2016). *Motivational interviewing in schools*. New York: Guilford Press.

Roth, A. D., & Pilling, S. (2007). *The competences required to deliver effective cognitive and behavioural therapy for people with depression and with anxiety disorders*. London: Department of Health.

18

MI processes – 2. Focusing

Rollnick, Kaplan and Rutschman (2016) offered a definition of focusing as "an observable process that describes how people in a conversation decide what change to talk about, and which direction the conversation should go in" (p. 29). Essentially it is about channelling the conversation so that the most useful and salient points to the client are addressed at any particular time. Miller and Rollnick (2013) likened focusing with the idea of creating an agenda for change.

Agenda-setting and -structuring sessions are also under-pinned by CBT technique and include the notion of negotiating a specific agenda with the client (Roth, 2016). This chapter will look at focusing within both MI and CBT, with a view to how it might be used most effectively in practice.

Finding the focus topic

Miller and Rollnick (2013) proposed that the focus for change could come from three sources:

1. The priorities and goals of the client
2. The context for the therapeutic interaction (e.g. smoking cessation, alcohol or drug rehabilitation)
3. Factors identified by the therapist which potentially affect the client's life significantly, but may not be immediately obvious to the client (e.g. the impact of cannabis use on a young person's education, or of non-adherence to treatment for a long-term health condition).

Miller and Rollnick (2013) suggested that rather than the therapist directing the client to a particular agenda, or completely following the client's priorities, that the therapist should use a guiding style to promote focusing. This is described as a "collaborative search for direction" (p. 99) in which topic areas emerge from discussions which address what the client would like to talk about, but also reference the expertise of the therapist and acknowledge the therapeutic context and the reasons for the client being there. Miller and Rollnick (2013) proposed three scenarios when thinking about focusing:

1. The focus is clear from the outset, perhaps because of a narrow brief for the therapeutic support.
2. There are a number of different possibilities to focus on. If this is the case, a technique called 'agenda mapping', described later in this chapter, can be useful.
3. The focus is unclear and work is required to develop a shared focus. Moving forward may also require clinical formulation by the therapist.

Roth (2016) highlighted that an indicator of therapeutic practice was whether the therapist shared responsibility for agenda setting and structuring the session with the client. This fits very much with the MI notion of collaboration and partnership (see Chapter 8).

Agenda mapping

Miller and Rollnick (2013, pp. 105–116) described the process of agenda mapping, which involves first listing a number of options for discussion. This can be done using a bubble chart, where a sheet containing blank bubbles is populated by the client, therapist, or during conversation, with possible topics for discussion. Through discussion, the topic areas are then considered and a focus area can be co-constructed. This approach could potentially complement a CBT agenda-setting process, cognisant of shared responsibility, appropriate pace and a flexible structure (Roth, 2016).

How to use focusing effectively

Gobat et al. (2018) identify three specific challenges involved in effective focusing:

1. Identifying and conceptualising different topics which might form the basis for discussion
2. Narrowing the focus in order to prioritise a single topic from this list of possible topics
3. Holding the focus on this topic in a way that helps facilitate change for the client in this area.

Gobat et al. (2018) developed the motivational interviewing focusing instrument (MIFI) from a systematic review of how focusing was evaluated in previous studies and coding of MI interactions. The instrument allows consideration of focusing behaviour across five domains:

(a) *Establishing focus* in a strategic and purposeful way
(b) *Holding focus* and attention to the topic
(c) *Developing depth and momentum*, making progress in understanding the client's perspective of the topic
(d) *Partnership* through conveying that wisdom and expertise lie with the client
(e) *Empathy* through attempting to understand the client's perspective.

Potentially considering these domains, either formally using the MIFI, or informally through personal reflection or professional supervision may be a way of enhancing and developing practice.

Practising focusing: practitioner reflection

The checklist shown in Figure 18.1 is designed to allow practitioner reflection on the skills associated with focusing and is based on previous literature (Atkinson & Woods, 2018; Gobat et al., 2018; Miller & Rollnick, 2013; Rollnick et al., 2016; Roth, 2016).

Focusing	Check ☐	Evidence
• I have established with which areas (if any) are most important to them in terms of potentially making a change.	☐	
• I have helped the client to identify and prioritise topics for discussion.[1]	☐	
• The client and I have a reasonable idea of the goals we are working towards.	☐	
• I have a developing understanding of the client's perspective on the topic.	☐	
• I have used appropriate structure and pace in relation to setting and following an agenda, bearing in mind the needs of the client.	☐	
• I have struck a balance between adhering to the structure of the agenda, whilst remaining flexible, and responsive to the client's needs.	☐	
• I have conveyed to the client that our work is a partnership and that they are the expert in their own situation, with regards to the topic.	☐	
• I am able to empathise with the client's predicament in relation to the topic(s) we are exploring.	☐	

Figure 18.1 Protocol for practitioner reflection on the engagement process within MICBT

1 Agenda setting and a bubble chart (Miller & Rollnick, 2013, p.110) can be a useful strategy for enabling this as it provides a visual record of possible topics for discussion.

Summary

1. Focusing and agenda setting is an important principle of both MI and CBT. It should be done in partnership with the client and the approach should be structured but responsive to their needs.
2. Using a bubble chart and undertaking agenda mapping can be one structured way of focusing change conversations.
3. Protocols including the MIFI can be used for practitioner self-reflection or within supervision.

References

Atkinson, C., & Woods, K. (2018). Integrity in the delivery of school-based motivational interviewing: protocols for practitioners. In McNamara, E. (Ed.), *Motivational interviewing with children and young people III: Education and community settings* (pp. 76–92). Ainsdale: Positive Behaviour Management.

Gobat, N., Copeland, L., Cannings-john, R., Robling, M., Carpenter, J., Cowley, L., … Sanders, J. (2018). "Focusing" in motivational interviewing: Development of a training tool for practitioners. *European Journal for Person Centered Healthcare*, 6(1), 37–49.

Miller, W. R., & Rollnick, S. (2013). *Motivational interviewing, third edition: Helping people change*. New York: Guilford Press.

Rollnick, S., Kaplan, S., & Rutschman, R. (2016). *Motivational interviewing in schools*. New York: Guilford Press.

Roth, A. D. (2016). A new scale for the assessment of competences in cognitive and behavioural therapy. *Behavioural and Cognitive Psychotherapy*, 44(5), 620–624. doi:10.1017/S1352465816000011

19

MI processes – 3. Evoking

The process of evoking change talk is at the very heart of MI practice, but how is this enabled? This chapter cites some of the significant literature focused on eliciting change talk and turns it into practical strategies. Further, focus is placed on how change talk can be amplified, extended and verbalised as commitment to change.

Importance and confidence of change

Miller and Rollnick (2013) highlighted the value of asking clients about how important change is to them and how confident they are that it is achievable. For example, a client might be desperate to stop using drugs, realising the effect it is having on his work, family and personal life; however, he might believe this to be impossible, given his physical dependence, peer group and life pressures. Assessment can be done using scaling, asking the client to rate their motivation or confidence on a scale of 0–10. Although this technique is not unique to MI, it gives the therapist an indication of how to move forward and whether the priority is to strengthen the client's motivation, or self-efficacy for change.

Reasons for and against change

Another potential opportunity for evoking change talk is to help the client explore reasons for and against change. Rollnick, Heather and Bell (1992) suggested asking clients to identify the "good things and the less good things" about a particular behaviour, avoiding terms such as "problem" or "concern" (p. 31). This strategy can offer information about the client's context and readiness for change. Additionally, it requires the client to be metacognitive and explicit about the reasons why a particular behaviour might be maintained. These may be more personal and specific than reasons for not changing, which may represent more widely held professional, societal or stereotypical views about the problems associated with a behaviour, such as those caused by not adhering to treatment, or arising from substance abuse.

Evoking change talk

Assessment of change is a useful starting point and gives the therapist a more accurate idea about how best to proceed, depending on the client's level of readiness. However, Miller and Rollnick (2013) highlighted the difference between verbalising intentions and actually changing behaviour, and that actually mobilising change talk is synonymous with clients being at the preparation or action phases of the TTM (see Chapter 7). However, they also described how MI as a process involves "literally talking oneself into change" (p. 168) and how this can be achieved through using the skills of MI.

Miller and Rollnick (2013) proposed a number of additional techniques that can be used to evoke change talk:

- *Querying extremes* – e.g. "What is the best/worst that could happen?"
- *Looking back* and finding exceptions when the behaviour did not occur, or occurred less; or exploring life before the behaviour started or became problematic.
- *Looking forward* and thinking about how life would be in a preferred future (e.g. "How would you like your life to be in five years' time?").
- *Exploring goals and values* (see Chapter 25).

- *Reasons and need for change.* As well as the desire or motivation, and perceptions of the client's ability to make change, Miller and Rollnick (2013) described the importance of understanding both the client's reasons for change and to what extent they feel that they need to change their behaviour. For example, if the client is anxious, reducing their symptoms might help them to resume work. However, is this something which imperative and what would be their reasons for returning to their job?
- *Sharing intentions of change.* Miller and Rollnick (1991) highlighted the importance of the client verbalising a plan, suggesting that the more a client is able to tell others of his or her intentions, the more the commitment to change is strengthened.

Why is evoking important in CBT?

CBT is potentially a very positive intervention for facilitating change and promoting positive mental health. However, Marker and Norton (2018) noted that even with its powerful evidence base, 15–50% of clients receiving CBT did not respond to treatment; while 23% of those receiving support for anxiety did not complete therapy. MI potentially offers a lens for considering why change would be necessary or important for clients who are not yet ready to fully engage with support. Understanding these nuances of motivation and how these potentially affect outcomes for the client is likely to improve the CBT formulation and to allow the therapist to target and refine the intervention more effectively.

Practitioner checklist

The checklist given in Figure 19.1 is developed from Atkinson and Woods (2018), Miller and Rollnick (2013) and Rollnick, Kaplan and Rutschman (2016) and can support practitioner reflection on their evoking practice.

Evoking	Check □	Evidence
• I have accepted ambivalence about change as normal.	□	
• I have noticed talk for change (change talk) and against change (sustain talk).	□	
• I have tried to draw from the client their ideas about how and why to change.	□	
• I have asked carefully worded questions to try and elicit change talk.	□	
• I have asked the client questions about importance and confidence (the "Why?" and "How?" of change).	□	
• I have asked the client about their reasons and need for change.	□	
• I have used reflections and summaries to feed change talk back to the client.	□	

Figure 19.1 Protocol for practitioner reflection on the evoking process within MICBT

Summary

1. Evoking is central to the notion of MI and offers a way of exploring clients' motivation and reasons *for* change, as well as their ability and need *to* change.
2. There are a number of different techniques and approaches which can help practitioners evoke motivation and reasons for change.
3. Evoking can be an important element of a MICBT intervention, particularly for clients who are finding it difficult to maintain engagement with therapy.

References

Atkinson, C., & Woods, K. (2018). Integrity in the delivery of school-based motivational interviewing: protocols for practitioners. In McNamara, E. (Ed.), *Motivational interviewing with children and young people III: Education and community settings* (pp. 76–92). Ainsdale: Positive Behaviour Management.

Marker, I., & Norton, P. J. (2018). The efficacy of incorporating motivational interviewing to cognitive behavior therapy for anxiety disorders: A review and meta-analysis. *Clinical Psychology Review*, *62*(April), 1–10. doi:10.1016/j.cpr.2018.04.004

Miller, W. R., & Rollnick, S. (1991). *Motivational interviewing: Preparing people to change addictive behaviour*. New York: Guilford Press.

Miller, W. R., & Rollnick, S. (2013). *Motivational interviewing, third edition: Helping people change*. New York: Guilford Press.

Rollnick, S., Heather, N., & Bell, A. (1992). Negotiating behaviour change in medical settings: The development of brief motivational interviewing. *Journal of Mental Health, 1*, 25–37. doi:10.3109/09638239209034509

Rollnick, S., Kaplan, S., & Rutschman, R. (2016). *Motivational interviewing in schools*. New York: Guilford Press.

20

MI processes – 4. Planning

Notably, Miller and Rollnick (2013) paid less attention to planning than to the other three processes, leading Lewis, Larson and Korcuska (2017) to claim that planning was the least well-defined of the four processes. Specifically, Miller and Rollnick (2013) proposed that MI is about moving people from ambivalence towards change and that they did not intend to provide a comprehensive programme for clients who were ready to change their behaviour. This chapter explores some of the techniques and approaches which can enhance planning, drawing particularly on CBT.

Entering the planning phase

Frey, Sims and Alvarez (2013) noted that MI can be implemented without planning, but stressed that engaging, focusing and evoking are essential. Miller and Rollnick (2013) claimed that once clients reach a stage of readiness for change, they will begin thinking and planning for change themselves and do not always require additional support. Indications of readiness for change include increased change talk and diminished sustain talk; the client envisioning, asking questions about and taking steps towards change; and resolution of ambivalence (Miller & Rollnick, 2013). In terms of making a plan, the way forward may be obvious, they may be several options, or a plan might have to be devised "from scratch" (Miller & Rollnick, 2013, p. 280).

Miller and Rollnick (2013) noted commitment to change can be strengthened by verbalising both intentions towards change and the specifics of an implementation plan. In the sections below, we explore specific methods which may support planning within MICBT.

A method of planning

Miller and Rollnick (2013) suggested using goal attainment scaling (GAS) as a way of planning for change, and this was later explored in greater depth by Lewis et al. (2017). GAS first involves the therapist and client identifying a "goal attainment guide" (Lewis et al., 2017, p. 199) by creating goals and behavioural indicators, which identify whether the client is achieving the goal or not. This is then used to determine the progress the client is making, typically via a five point scale, from −2 to +2, with a midpoint of zero, which defines the expected outcome. Behavioural descriptions, specific to the goal, are provided for each of the points. Lewis et al. (2017) suggested using this approach, within the spirit of MI and employing OARS skills to enhance the planning process for clients.

Planning in MICBT

There are a lot of techniques in CBT which could be combined with MI planning to support a client-led intervention for behavioural change. These include exposure techniques, guided self-help, exposure techniques, applied relaxation and tension, and activity monitoring and scheduling (Roth & Pilling, 2007). Boyer, Geurts and Prins (2015) described an MICBT intervention for adolescents with attention deficit hyperactivity disorder, which incorporated elements of CBT, MI and GAS. It is presented here as an adapted set of steps, which could be incorporated into planning within MICBT practice.

1. Devise a goal attainment guide using GAS.
2. Review progress at the start of each session using the guide.
3. Explore progress in relation to the goals within the spirit of MI.
4. Agree on a homework "experiment" linked to the goals for the forthcoming period, before the next session, which should be client-led.

5. Evaluate the usefulness of the session with regard to its importance, usefulness and the likelihood of the client trying the homework "experiment".

6. Emphasis the autonomy of the client to practise the plan. If motivation appears low, this may be an indicator that readiness for change needs to be reviewed, or that the client has not been in charge of the change plan.

Practitioner checklist

As with the other processes, effective planning can be developed through reflective practice and supervision. Key elements of MI planning are incorporated within the grid below which may be helpful in supporting the process. The checklist in Figure 20.1 is derived from planning ideas proposed by Atkinson and Woods (2018), Miller and Rollnick (2013) and Rollnick, Kaplan and Rutschman (2016).

Focusing	Check ☐	Evidence
• I have been cautious not to jump ahead with the planning process and continue to be accepting of ambivalence.	☐	
• I have affirmed and reflected stronger change talk.	☐	
• I have asked the client about their readiness for change.	☐	
• I have asked open questions to try and help the client to make their plan more concrete and specific.	☐	
• I have helped the client to think about possible change options to allow them different choices.	☐	

Figure 20.1 Protocol for practitioner reflection on the planning process within MICBT

- I have reflected and reinforced the client's commitment to change. ☐
- I have encouraged the client to share decisions about changes with others and to keep a record of success. ☐
- I have helped the client to think about any slips as learning opportunities. ☐
- I have helped the client think about any possible barriers to change and ways of seeking support should these arise ☐

Figure 20.1 (Continued)

Summary

1. MI planning is arguably less well-defined that the other processes.
2. CBT approaches can be useful in enhancing MI planning practice.
3. GAS delivered in an MI-adherent way is a potentially useful approach for planning for change.
4. Defining competencies and using practitioner checklists can improve practice through reflection and supervision.

References

Atkinson, C., & Woods, K. (2018). Integrity in the delivery of school-based motivational interviewing: protocols for practitioners. In McNamara, E. (Ed.), *Motivational interviewing with children and young people III: Education and community settings* (pp. 76–92). Ainsdale: Positive Behaviour Management.

Boyer, B. E., Geurts, H. M., & Prins, P. J. M. (2015). Two novel CBTs for adolescents with ADHD : the value of planning skills. *European Child & Adolescent Psychiatry*, *24*, 1075–1090. doi:10.1007/s00787-014-0661-5

Frey, A. J., Sims, K., & Alvarez, M. E. (2013). The promise of motivational interviewing for securing a niche in the RtI movement. *Children & Schools, 35*(2), 67–70. doi:10.1093/cs/cdt004

Lewis, T. F., Larson, M. F., & Korcuska, J. S. (2017). Strengthening the planning process of motivational interviewing using goal attainment scaling. *Journal of Mental Health Counselling, 39*(3), 195–210. doi:10.17744/mehc.39.3.02

Miller, W. R., & Rollnick, S. (2013). *Motivational interviewing, third edition: Helping people change.* New York: Guilford Press.

Rollnick, S., Kaplan, S., & Rutschman, R. (2016). *Motivational interviewing in schools.* New York: Guilford Press.

Roth, A. D., & Pilling, S. (2007). *The competences required to deliver effective cognitive and behavioural therapy for people with depression and with anxiety disorders.* London: Department of Health.

21

MI skills – 1. Open questions

Why are open questions important?

Broadly speaking, open questions are those that allow people to provide whatever information they want, rather than request a specific response (often "yes" or "no"). Open questions fit well with the spirit of MI, as they allow the client to present information which is important to them in as much detail as they choose. They allow a wide range of answers and may seek information, invite the client's perspective or encourage self-exploration (Apodaca et al., 2016). Open-ended questions can also include exploring the pros and cons of a particular behaviour (Laws et al., 2018).

Open questions are associated with both more change and more sustain talk. This is probably because they allow exploration of issues, as well as motivational enhancement (e.g. identifying barriers to change through identifying the 'good things' about a particular behaviour) (Laws et al., 2018).

What sort of open questions can I ask?

Rollnick, Heather and Bell (1992) developed a brief MI approach to support practitioners who wanted a clearer sense of direction when undertaking MI. Within their 'menu of strategies', they used a number of open questioning techniques, as shown in Table 21.1. Excerpts may be helpful in offering examples of the types of direction a therapist can take in using open-ended questions. In the following example, the behaviour in question is substance use.

Table 21.1 Examples of open questions within a brief motivational interview (adapted from Rollnick et al., 1992)

Approach	Open questioning techniques
Opening discussion (general)	General discussion about the client's current lifestyle, situation and stresses. Possible questions might include: • How do you see things? • How do you feel about us talking about your use of _____?
Opening discussion (health and substance use)	Where there is concern about the impact of substance use, on the client's health, a general, open-ended question about their health can be followed up by more specific questioning, for example: • Where does your use of _____ fit in? • How does you use of _____ affect your health?
A typical day/ session	This line of question asks, without judgement, or reference to 'problems' or concerns for an open-ended description of the client's lifestyle and can provide "A wealth of information related to the assessment" (Rollnick et al., 1992, p. 30). After a typical or recent day has been identified, a suggested question is: • Can we spend the next 5–10 minutes going through this day from beginning to end? What happened? How did you feel and how did your use of _____ fit in? Let's start at the beginning...
The good things and the less good things	This approach helps the therapist understand more about the client's feelings about the behaviour in question, using the following prompts: • What are some of the good things about your use of _____? • What are some of the less good things about your use of _____?
The future and the present	For clients with some degree of concern about a behaviour, thinking about future aspirations can help create dissonance about the current situation, for example: • How would you like things to be different in the future?

Closed questions in MI

In the past, one indicator of proficiency in MI has been the balance of open and closed questions (those that typically prompt a short, specific response). Moyers, Martin, Manuel, Miller and Ernst (2010) suggested that MI competency was evident if 70% of the questions were open, although this ratio is not a feature of the most recent edition of the Motivational Interviewing Treatment Integrity (MITI) scale (Moyers, Manuel, & Ernst, 2014). Miller and Rollnick (2013) suggested that overuse of closed questions can stifle engagement and assert a notion of the therapist as expert. Additionally, closed questions can limit answers, restrict the client's narrative and indicate that the therapist rather than the client is setting the agenda for change.

Miller and Rollnick (2013) note that closed questions can be useful in checking things out with the client (e.g. "Have I understood you correctly?"; "So can I just check that's what you're planning to do?"). It is important to note that closed questions are not 'off limits' and can be helpful, particularly when used within the spirit of MI.

Questioning in CBT

According to Roth and Pilling (2007) the main questioning approach mentioned within core CBT competencies is Socratic questioning. Paul and Elder (2007) describe how Socratic questioning is "systemic, disciplined and deep and usually focuses on foundational concepts, principles, theories, issues, or problems" (p. 36). Neenan (2009) suggested that CBT therapists have different ideas about what Socratic questioning actually is, which relate to the extent to which they perceive their aim as, to change minds or to guide discovery (Padesky, 1993). To some extent, this perspective would determine to what extent their CBT approach is consistent with MI. Padesky (1993, p. 4) offered the following definition of Socratic questioning (Figure 21.1):

115

Socratic questioning involves asking the client questions which:

a) The client has the knowledge to answer;
b) Draw the client's attention to information which is relevant to the issue being discussed but which may be outside the client's current focus;
c) Generally move from the concrete to the more abstract so that;
d) The client can, in the end, apply the new information to either re-evaluate a previous conclusion or construct a new idea.

Figure 21.1 Socratic questioning

None of these ideas make Socratic questioning inconsistent with MI questioning. However, CBT practitioners wishing to practise within the spirit of MI may wish to reflect on the extent to which the process is client-led (guided discovery) rather than therapist-led (changing minds). Using open questions and reflection can help the therapist to follow the client's agenda, rather than trying to impose their own process for change.

Summary

1. Open questions lead to change talk and behavioural exploration. Closed questions potentially narrow the focus of discussion and can mean the agenda for change lies with the therapist.
2. Monitoring the balance of open and closed questions can be a way for MICBT practitioners to reflect on practice and develop their competency.
3. CBT practitioners using Socratic questioning could use the notion of open questions in MI to think about the extent to which they are trying to guide discovery, or change minds.

References

Apodaca, T. R., Jackson, K. M., Borsari, B., Magill, M., Longabaugh, R., Mastroleo, N. R., & Barnett, N. P. (2016). Which individual therapist behaviors elicit client change talk and sustain talk in motivational interviewing? *Journal of Substance Abuse Treatment*, *61*, 60–65. doi:10.1016/j.jsat.2015.09.001

Laws, M. B., Magill, M., Mastroleo, N. R., Gamarel, K. E., Howe, C. J., Walthers, J., … Kahler, C. W. (2018). A sequential analysis of motivational interviewing technical skills and client responses. *Journal of Substance Abuse Treatment*, *92*, 27–34. doi:10.1016/j.jsat.2018.06.006

Miller, W. R., & Rollnick, S. (2013). *Motivational interviewing, third edition: Helping people change*. New York: Guilford Press.

Moyers, T. B., Manuel, J. K., & Ernst, D. (2014). Motivational Interviewing Treatment Integrity Coding Manual 4.1 (MITI 4.1), (December). Retrieved from http://casaa.unm.edu/download/MITI4_1.pdf

Moyers, T. B., Martin, T., Manuel, J. K., Miller, W. R., & Ernst, D. (2010). *Revised Global Scales: Motivational Interviewing Treatment Integrity 3.1.1 (MITI 3.1.1)*. University of New Mexico: Center on Alcoholism, Substance Abuse and Addictions (CASAA). Retrieved from http://www.motivationalinterview.org/Documents/miti3_1.pdf

Neenan, M. (2009). Using Socratic questioning in coaching. *Journal of Rational-Emotive and Cognitive-Behavior Therapy*, *27*(4), 249–264. doi:10.1007/s10942-007-0076-z

Padesky, C. A. (1993). Socratic questioning: Changing minds or guiding discovery. A Keynote Address Delivered at the European Congress of Behavioural and Cognitive Therapies, Vol. 24. Retrieved from http://padesky.com/newpad/wp-content/uploads/2012/11/socquest.pdf

Paul, R., & Elder, L. (2007). Critical thinking: the art of Socratic questioning. *Journal of Developmental Education*, *31*(1), 36–37.

Rollnick, S., Heather, N., & Bell, A. (1992). Negotiating behaviour change in medical settings: The development of brief motivational interviewing. *Journal of Mental Health*, *1*, 25–37. doi:10.3109/09638239209034509

Roth, A. D., & Pilling, S. (2007). The competences required to deliver effective cognitive and behavioural therapy for people with depression and with anxiety disorders. London: Department of Health.

22

MI skills – 2. Affirmations

What are affirmations?

Miller and Rollnick (2013) described the second skill of affirmations as a way of accentuating what is positive as well as to support and encourage. Affirmations are statements recognising the client's values, strengths, skills, efforts, behaviours and achievements. There is evidence that their use improves client outcomes (Romano & Peters, 2016), while significantly research by Apodaca et al. (2016) indicated that affirmations was the only MI skill which both increased change talk *and* reduced sustain talk.

Despite the importance of affirmations, they are often a skill overlooked in both MI practice and training. Part of the reason for this might be that affirming is a difficult skill to perform well. Miller and Rollnick (2013) stressed that, not only should affirmations be genuine, but that they should be statements that are true about the person. In the sections below, some key principles for considering how to affirm effectively are offered.

Get to know the client

Providing effective affirmations requires listening carefully to develop an understanding of the client because "You cannot honestly affirm what you do not know and appreciate" (Miller & Rollnick, 2013, p. 64). If affirmations are not delivered from this basis, they might be perceived as insincere, false or patronising, which may have a negative impact on the therapeutic relationship. This also means that it is important, during the process of engaging the client, to ask open-ended questions which elicit strengths, skills and attributes, alongside questions about the behaviour which is causing concern.

Be specific and evidence-based

Moyers, Manuel, and Ernst (2014) clarified that affirmations are not just about approval, "cheerleading" or non-specific praising. While there can be a place within therapy for a generally positive response, these behaviours should not be over-used and affirmations themselves and should be explicitly linked to client behaviours and/or characteristics. Additionally, affirmations are more authentic if you can provide the client with evidence to justify them. For example, saying "I can tell you are really smart, from the way you are taking time to consider your options" might be more meaningful to the client than "you are really smart".

Using affirmations is a difficult skill and depends on really getting to know the client, looking for their skills and strengths *or* attributes and values, and then genuinely affirming thoughts or behaviours towards change. In Figures 22.1 and 22.2, there are examples of first how to affirm behaviour and effort and second how to affirm strengths and values.

Client:	I've really put on weight since I started taking this medication but I'm trying to eat healthy and exercise.
Therapist:	You are really trying out lots of things to manage your weight and health, even though it's a struggle.
Client:	I nearly just stayed in bed today.
Therapist:	You didn't want to come here today, but you did it anyway, I really appreciate the effort that has taken.
Client:	I mostly manage to eat right, but sometimes too much drink upsets my blood sugar.
Therapist:	Managing your diabetes well is something you know a lot about and is something you're really trying to do.

Figure 22.1 Affirmations for behaviours or efforts

Client:	I'm not ready right now to do this but if I decide to do something I usually do it.
Therapist:	You are a strong-willed person and when you put your mind to things you are able to see them through.
Client:	I got into fight because they'd had a go at my friend.
Therapist:	You are the kind of person who cares a lot for other people and is loyal to his friends.
Client:	I still get up and take the kids to school even when I'm feeling really low.
Therapist:	Being a good mum and making sure your kids get an education is really important to you.
Client:	I'm still smoking weed but I managed to stop for six months last year.
Therapist:	You know you are someone who can stop smoking weed, you did it last year, which shows you have the ability to do it again.
Client:	I burst out laughing yesterday when the electric bill came through. I just can't pay it.
Therapist:	Even though things are difficult you have kept your sense of humour.

Figure 22.2 Affirmations for strengths or values

Encourage the client to self-affirm

Miller and Rollnick (2013) noted that not all affirmations need to come from the therapist, and through careful and sensitive questions, clients can be enabled to identify their own strengths, successes and endeavours. Naar and Safren (2017) suggested that when using MICBT homework activities, prompts can be used which identify aspects that went well between sessions, as well as skills and attributes which can support progress. These can then be highlighted and re-emphasised during the next therapy session.

Notice the client's response

Miller and Rollnick (2013) highlighted that cultural factors may influence the client's response to affirmations. Furthermore, this may be affected by a myriad of other factors including the client's personality, previous experience, social network and current context. Miller and Rollnick (2013) emphasised that "As with all of MI, the client is your guide" (p. 66). Be attentive to how the client responds to affirmations and to what approaches seem most successful. Keeping the conversation light-hearted and using humour can reduce resistance, if the client finds it difficult to accept affirmations. Finally, if an affirmation is not well-received by the client, acknowledge this and reflect it back (e.g. "that doesn't sound like a good description of you").

Reframing

The CBT skill of reframing may offer possibilities for providing affirmations, and within this, opportunities for cognitive restructuring. Used sensitively, affirmations can be used to restructure aspects of the client's life that they perceive negatively. For example, "I'm always being led astray by other people" could be reframed as "You enjoy the company of others and like being part of a group, although this can make recovery difficult." Often people's fallibilities are also their strengths, and recognising this can potentially help clients redirect these attributes into more positive behaviours.

Developing proficiency in using affirmations

Moyers, Manuel, and Ernst (2014) include affirmations as part of the Motivational Interviewing Treatment Integrity (MITI) coding process. This can be used by supervisors or colleagues developmentally to review practice and identify targets for developing proficiency. Moyers et al. (2014) note that clinicians can overuse positive statements (e.g. "awesome", "wonderful", "fabulous"). The MITI only credits these as affirmations on the first two or three occasions. After that, an affirmation is only coded when the therapist's statement is genuine, positive and specific. Reviewing affirmation practice in this way is potentially beneficial to both the reviewer and the reviewee.

Summary

Giving affirmations is an extremely important, yet often overlooked skill in MI practice and training. In giving affirmations, it is useful to try and consider the following points.

1. Get to know the client so that your affirmations can be genuine.
2. Try and make your affirmations specific and relevant.
3. Encourage the client to make self-affirmations.
4. Be attentive to the way in which affirmations are received, and adjust your responses accordingly.
5. Look for opportunities to reframe attributes, to promote cognitive restructuring.
6. Revisit and re-evaluate this area of your MICBT practice on a regular basis.

References

Apodaca, T. R., Jackson, K. M., Borsari, B., Magill, M., Longabaugh, R., Mastroleo, N. R., & Barnett, N. P. (2016). Which individual therapist behaviors elicit client change talk and sustain talk in motivational interviewing? *Journal of Substance Abuse Treatment, 61*, 60–65. doi:10.1016/j.jsat.2015.09.001

Miller, W. R., & Rollnick, S. (2013). *Motivational interviewing, third edition: Helping people change*. New York: Guilford Press.

Moyers, T. B., Manuel, J. K., & Ernst, D. (2014). Motivational Interviewing Treatment Integrity Coding Manual 4.1 (MITI 4.1), (December). Retrieved from http://casaa.unm.edu/download/MITI4_1.pdf

Naar, S., & Safren, S. A. (2017). *Motivational interviewing and CBT: Combining strategies for maximum effectiveness*. New York: Guilford Press.

Romano, M., & Peters, L. (2016). Understanding the process of motivational interviewing: A review of the relational and technical hypotheses. *Psychotherapy Research: Journal of the Society for Psychotherapy Research*, *26*(2), 220–240. doi:10.1080/10503307.2014.954154

23

MI skills – 3. Reflections

Reflective listening is central to MI practice. This chapter will start by describing why reflective listening is so important within the therapeutic relationship. It will then move on to describing some different ways of using reflections, before considering implications for MICBT practice.

The importance of reflective listening

Miller (2018) devoted an entire textbook to the art of empathic listening, highlighting the importance of accurate empathy, seeking to understand the meaning behind the spoken word, and addressing what he termed 'roadblocks' to listening. These typically referred to behaviours which were indicative of the therapist following their own agenda rather than the client's, including advising, persuading, judging or moralising. While forming reflective listening statements is just one element of empathic listening, it is an important skill in that it communicates to the client that they are being heard and understood.

Reflective listening resides at the very heart of MI. While it is not always easy to learn, with practice, reflections become more natural and straightforward. The next sections will offer some different ways of offering reflections and provide tips for improving practice.

Simple and complex reflections

Miller and Rollnick (2013) described how reflecting involves responding to client talk with a statement rather than a question.

A simple reflection would typically convey that the therapist has understood the client, without going much beyond the content of their words, for example:

> **Client:** On the days when work is stressful, I tend to drink more.
>
> **Therapist:** Drinking tends to be heavier on stressful days. A complex reflection is essentially an informed guess at the meaning behind the client's words, which would add substantial meaning or emphasis to the client's words. For example, a complex reflection to the client's statement above might be:
>
> **Therapist:** Drinking is a way of managing the demands of your job.

Overshooting and undershooting

Overshooting and undershooting are two specific types of reflection which can be used to elicit the client's emotional response to situations. Undershooting involves deliberately underplaying the strength of feeling linked to the client's words. For example, if a client was to say, "I hate my husband", an undershooting response might be "Your relationship isn't going too well at the moment". This might elicit a stronger response from the client, such as "Well that's an understatement. Most of the time I feel like killing him!" Alternatively an overshooting response might be "Nothing is going well in your relationship". This might elicit further detail, such as "Well he's trying hard to find work, but then he just ends up going out with his mates and leaving me to do everything." Miller and Rollnick (2013) suggest erring on the side of undershooting, as if the intensity of an emotion is under-represented, people tend to continue exploring it.

Double-sided reflection

Remember our notion of ambivalence being like an internal committee (see Chapter 2)? A double-sided reflection is a way of reflecting both change and sustain talk in the same sentence, for example:

Client:	I do think using cannabis is making me more paranoid, but it's what I do when I'm with my partner and my friends.
Therapist:	You're considering reducing your cannabis use because of the impact on your mental health, but you're worried about how it might affect your relationship and social life.

Careful reframing and restructuring

CBT therapists will be well-practised in the use of reframing and restructuring to help clients deal with maladaptive or problematic thoughts. However, if the emphasis is to correct phenomena associated with emotional distress (Dobson, 2007) the client might lose their sense of agency and autonomy, and the CBT might feel more like 'treatment' than a talking therapy in which the client is seen as an equal partner. Although reframing can offer a different perspective or meaning for the client, it should not be a case of arguing about the correct perception, but about inviting the client to see things from a different angle (Miller & Rollnick, 2013).

Managing discord

Acknowledging the point above, Miller and Rollnick (2013) advised therapists to become attuned to when interactions might represent the therapist's preferred course of action, rather than respecting the client's situation and recognising their ability to act in their own best interests. Signs that the process is not working well for the client include defensive statements, the client taking an oppositional stance, interrupting or disengagement. Where there is discord, Miller and Rollnick (2013) advocated that reflection is the best tool for re-establishing the therapeutic alliance, for example:

Client:	I'm fed up with this. Maybe I just drink a lot because I like drinking. Maybe it's got nothing to do with the way I think about things.
Therapist:	That formulation doesn't sound as if it's helpful to you. Tell me about some of the reasons why you like drinking.

Tips for reflecting

When therapists start practising MI, we find that many are shocked by just how many questions they ask. Previous Motivational Interviewing Treatment Integrity (MITI) guidance (Moyers, Martin, Manuel, Miller, & Ernst, 2010) suggested competent therapists used a ratio of two reflections to every question, and although this specific figure has been removed from more recent versions, the authors still see this as a useful notional ratio by which to evaluate practice.

For therapists used to asking questions, Miller and Rollnick (2013) suggested that almost any question could be turned into a reflective statement. Guidance offered suggests thinking of the question you might be intending to ask. For example, if a client says, "I've been trying to organise myself for a job interview, but I can't seem to get out of the door?" the therapist might really want to ask: "What's stopping you?" However, the same line of enquiry could be pursued by offering a reflection such as: "You've taken lots of steps towards preparing, but it sounds like some things are getting in the way".

Miller and Rollnick (2013) also advised on the tone of voice. Inflecting your voice up can mean that even the most carefully constructed reflection effectively becomes a question. Instead, inflect your voice downward. This too will take some practice.

Effective reflecting is not an easy skill and one which takes time to learn. However, it should be noted that MICBT is not about finding the perfect reflection. Empathic listening, interest in the client's view, respect for their autonomy and practising within the spirit of MI (Chapter 8) will go a long way to ensuring that that the client feels valued, respected and listened to.

Summary

1. There are different approaches to offering reflections within MICBT, but all are based on empathic listening and acting within the spirit of MI.
2. Where discord within the therapeutic relationship is perceived, reflective listening can be useful in re-establishing the therapeutic alliance.
3. Noticing your own practice, and starting to use reflections where you might have previously asked a question are good starting points for improving your reflective listening skills.

References

Dobson, K. S. (Ed). (2007). *Handbook of cognitive-behavioral therapies.* 3rd edition. London: Guildford Press.

Miller, W. R. (2018). *Listening well: The art of empathic understanding.* Eugene, OR: WIPF & Stock.

Miller, W. R., & Rollnick, S. (2013). *Motivational interviewing, third edition: Helping people change.* New York: Guilford Press.

Moyers, T. B., Martin, T., Manuel, J. K., Miller, W. R., & Ernst, D. (2010). *Revised Global Scales: Motivational Interviewing Treatment Integrity 3.1.1 (MITI 3.1.1)*. University of New Mexico: Center on Alcoholism, Substance Abuse and Addictions (CASAA). Retrieved from http://www.motivationalinterview.org/Documents/miti3_1.pdf

24

MI skills – 4. Summaries

The last of the four OARS skills is summaries. This chapter will offer some tips for providing meaningful summaries to clients. It will explore why summarising is important and will consider how effective summarising can enhance effective MICBT practice.

Using summaries with MICBT

Miller and Rollnick (2013) described how summaries are essentially reflections that pull together several things that the client has told you. "Using summaries and feedback to structure the session" is a core competency within CBT (Roth & Pilling, 2007, p. 12), with the authors advocating for summaries based on careful listening, as well as periodic and explicit 'capsule' summaries – a way of presenting information in shortened form – which help to structure the session.

So what makes a good summary? Within their document designed to assess core CBT skills, Muse, Mcmanus, Rakovshik and Kennerley (2014) proposed four levels of competency in using reflective summaries – from 'limited' to 'advanced'. Notably a high level of skill would see therapists using summaries at the beginning and end of the session as well as appropriate and regular intervals during the session. Summaries would be clear, succinct and based on information elicited from the client through skilful questioning. Capsule summaries would be meaningful and draw together salient information and key learning points to facilitate a joint understanding of important information, leading the client towards new insights and readiness for change.

While this seems like excellent tangible guidance, arguably as with other 'generic' features of counselling (Driessen & Hollon, 2011), summaries are better defined within MI than within other therapeutic approaches. Specifically, Miller and Rollnick (2013) suggested that person-centred counselling offers little guidance on what to include within summaries and what to leave out. The following sections offer therapist guidance for effective summaries, based on extensive guidance from Miller and Rollnick (2013).

Choosing the content of summaries

Summaries require the therapist to make a choice about what to include or highlight, and what to leave out. Some of the content of summaries will be determined by the sort of summary that is being used, with Miller and Rollnick (2013) identifying three distinct categories – *collecting, linking* and *transitional*. These are identified and described in Table 24.1, with examples given for each.

Table 24.1 Different types of summaries in MI (adapted from Miller & Rollnick, 2013)

Type of summary	Description	Example
Collecting summary	Collects together information about a particular discussion point.	"So it sounds as if some of things you have noticed recently about your drug use are that it might be increasing; that on a couple of occasions it has led you into situations where you have done things you've later not feel so good about; and that it has led to your partner starting to worry."

(Continued)

Type of summary	Description	Example
Linking summary	Links something that the client has said to something from a previous conversation.	"It's great that you found a way to manage your anxiety in that situation because you were concerned about the impact of your distress on your children. It's made me remember when you talked before about being a good parent and prioritising your children's needs over everything else."
Transitional summary	Pulls together important information, typically at the end of a task or session. The summary can also reflect ambivalence.	"You're wondering whether to stop going out with that group quite so much. They're lots of fun and you've known them for years. It would impact your social life. On the other side, it's pretty tricky to put any sort of parameters on your drinking when you're with them, which is causing a bit of tension at home… and your relationship is important to you. You're weighing up what to do."

When using a *collecting summary*, Miller and Rollnick (2013) suggested that the client should be invited to contribute to the summary. In the example in Table 24.1, a prompt such as "Anything else you've noticed?" could be used as many times as needed, until the list is exhaustive. All types of summaries can include affirmations, as in the *linking* example, both of client attributes, strengths and values, and of therapist's confidence in change, should the client wish to take action. In relation to *transitional summaries,* a possible phrase to include might be something like "I'm confident that if you decide to make a change in this part of your life, you'll find a way to do it!" (Berg-Smith, 2014, p. 114).

What is the purpose of summaries?

Miller and Rollnick (2013) suggest that summaries are different from reflections (see Chapter 23) in that they

- pull together a number of elements for the client;
- allow clients to hear different parts of their own experience simultaneously;
- help to summarise and therefore help the client to explore ambivalence;
- provide the client with a picture of why they might be "stuck";
- offer neutrality within the counselling relationship;
- are a good way of highlighting reasons for, and optimism about change;
- can help summarise a plan if the client is at this stage (see Chapter 20).

Offering written summaries

There may also be value in summarising information in written format (Kittles & Atkinson, 2009) in a way that outlines ambivalence, presents options for change and promotes client autonomy. Within written communication, Cordingley (2018) suggested building motivation through communicating empathy, increasing self-efficacy and communicating in a hopeful and collaborative tone. Information should be personalised. Communication could be between sessions or after the end of the therapy, and could be via different media, including letters, postcards and emails (Dunsmuir & Hardy, 2016).

Summary

1. Summaries are a way of pulling together information for the client.
2. One of the purposes of summaries can be to help the client reflect on ambivalence about change.

References

Berg-Smith, S. M. (2014). The art of teaching motivational interviewing. Retrieved from https://motivationalinterviewing.org/sites/default/files/the_art_of_teaching_mi_1.2.pdf

Cordingley, L. (2018). *Guiding principles for writing in an MI style.* Manchester, 28 February: Presentation to the Manchester Motivational Interviewing Network. Retrieved from https://docs.wixstatic.com/ugd/79e42a_f0d8828db5a0433e9a4e6b9066c4d854.pdf

Driessen, E., & Hollon, S. D. (2011). Motivational interviewing from a cognitive behavioral perspective. *Cognitive and Behavioral Practice, 18*(1), 70–73. doi:10.1016/j.cbpra.2010.02.007

Dunsmuir, S., & Hardy, J. (2016). *Delivering psychological therapies in schools and communities.* Leicester: BPS.

Kittles, M., & Atkinson, C. (2009). The usefulness of motivational interviewing as a consultation and assessment tool for working with young people. *Pastoral Care in Education, 27*(3), 241–254. doi:10.1080/02643940903133870

Miller, W. R., & Rollnick, S. (2013). *Motivational interviewing, third edition: Helping people change.* New York: Guilford Press.

Muse, K., Mcmanus, F., Rakovshik, S., & Kennerley, H. (2014). Assessment of Core CBT Skills (ACCS) Scale contributors, (July). Retrieved from www.accs-scale.co.uk

Roth, A. D., & Pilling, S. (2007). *The competences required to deliver effective cognitive and behavioural therapy for people with depression and with anxiety disorders.* London: Department of Health.

25

Exploring values, goals and aspirations

Understanding a client's values core values and aspirations provides the therapist with a unique perspective on their situation and potential reasons for change. In this chapter, practical strategies for ascertaining values, including interviews and card sorts, as well as overlaps with strengths-based approaches and CBT practice, are explored.

Miller and Rollnick (2013) highlighted the key role that appreciating a client's core values can play in therapy. They are a way of understanding the client's world view, which in turn can help the therapist gain accurate empathy. They can help identify the client's sense of meaning and purpose, what they aspire to and what goals they have. From a humanistic perspective, Wagner and Sanchez (2002) proposed that exploring values can help a client define their "ideal self".

The sections below will explore different ways of exploring values and goals within MI. Finally, the chapter will explore values within CBT practice and signpost additional resources, which may be useful to therapists.

Wagner and Sanchez (2002) proposed that values broadly fell into two types: *behavioural ideals* and *preferences for experiences* (p. 284). Behavioural ideals are judgements about what is good and not good and are consistent with beliefs (e.g. "family life is important"). Preferences for experiences are the values which guide clients to seeking situations they would like for themselves (e.g. "I would like to be a parent").

Miller and Rollnick (2013) suggested that values could be explored in both an open-ended and structured way. These two approaches will now be considered in turn.

Open-ended exploration of values

This approach can be used within MICBT-based conversations to elicit goals or values that clients may have internalised. Appropriate open-ended questions might be introduced, for example:

- What are some of the things in your life which are most important to you?
- Tell me what you would like your life to be like in five years' time.
- It sounds as if being a reliable and valued work colleague is an important value to you. What are some of your other important values?

Other OARS skills of affirmations, reflections and summaries can then be used to allow the client to explore these ideas further.

Structured exploration of values

Miller and Rollnick (2013) suggested a card-sorting activity could be used to identify values, and developed 100 value cards, which can be accessed via www.guilford.com/p/miller2. These can be organised, using Q-sort principles, into five piles labelled: Not Important, Somewhat Important, Important, Very Important and Most Important. Bean, Mazzeo, Stern, Bowen and Ingersoll (2011), who developed a values-based MI intervention to support adolescents with weight management, proposed that once the most important values had been selected, meaning could be explored further using the following type of questioning (p. 670):

- You said that [value] is important to you. What does [value] mean to you?
- How do you know in your daily life that [value] is important?
- How does [value] relate to [behaviour in question]?

Miller and Rollnick (2013) suggested that spending time exploring clients' top five to ten values helps the therapist develop an understanding of what it important to them and what is potentially motivating. Once again, OARS skills can help explore these values in a systematic and client-centred manner.

MI and strengths-based practice

Manthey, Knowles, Asher and Wahab (2011) described significant overlap between MI and strengths-based practice. In their open access article (see the References), they described how a combined MI/strengths-based approach could help elicit strengths, desires and aspirations, and past resources which could be used to support progress towards these goals. Manthey et al. (2011) provided a case example of how this structure could be used to audit strengths and help prioritise goals. A hypothetical example, adapted from Manthey et al. (2011), is shown in Table 25.1.

A number of different areas can be explored in this way. For example, Manthey et al. (2011) also considered financial assets, supportive relationships, wellness/health, leisure/recreational and spiritual/cultural factors, but these would be areas relevant to the client.

Values-based approaches within CBT

Although not an area emphasised strongly within CBT, some derivations of CBT have a more sophisticated approach to using values and goals within therapy. For example, acceptance and commitment therapy (ACT) pays considerable attention to identifying, assessing and clarifying values (see Harris, 2009 for extensive practical and workable examples). Furthermore, ACT sees values as being integral to the client's chosen direction and aims to direct people towards values as a way of moving towards

Table 25.1 A strengths-based assessment example

	Current strengths	Desires and aspirations What do I want in life?	Past resources – personal, social and environmental
Home/daily living	Rents a flat. Good relationship with housing association.	"I want to move out of this neighbourhood to somewhere where we can make a fresh start."	Showed persistence in getting this property.
	Keeps home tidy and makes sure that all children's needs are catered for. Good parent.	"Eventually I'd like a place of my own – a family home."	Determined once puts mind to things.
Education/ employment	Capable and articulate.	"I have thought about going back to college"	Did well at school.
	Good literacy and numeracy skills.		Has qualifications which could be useful in gaining employment.
	Creative and artistic.	"I'd like to do something practical – maybe making things"	Has had experience of retail and bar work – customer-facing jobs

goals. Guidance offered within this branch of therapy extends beyond Miller and Rollnick's (2013) description of using values and could be used to supplement work in this area.

Summary

1. Exploring values is a useful approach within MICBT. It helps build rapport, establish the client's world view, foster empathy and elicit reasons for change.
2. Values exploration can be unstructured, or structured. Structured approaches include card sorts, strengths-based assessment and using ACT approaches.

References

Bean, M. K., Mazzeo, S. E., Stern, M., Bowen, D., & Ingersoll, K. (2011). A values-based Motivational Interviewing (MI) intervention for pediatric obesity: Study design and methods for MI Values. *Contemporary Clinical Trials, 32*(5), 667–674. doi:10.1016/j.cct.2011.04.010

Harris, R. (2009). *The complete set of client handouts and worksheets from ACT books.* Oakland, CA: Harbinger. Retrieved from www.newharbinger.com

Manthey, T. J., Knowles, B., Asher, D., & Wahab, S. (2011). Strengths-based practice and motivational interviewing. *Advances in Social Work, 12*(2), 126–151.

Miller, W. R., & Rollnick, S. (2013). *Motivational interviewing, third edition: Helping people change.* New York: Guilford Press.

Wagner, C. C., & Sanchez, F. P. (2002). The role of values in motivational interviewing. In W. R. Miller & S. Rollnick (Eds.), *Motivational interviewing, second edition: Preparing people for change* (pp. 284–298). New York: Guilford Press.

26

Providing information

Given what we know about evolutionary theory (see Chapter 3 and de Almeida Neto [2017]) it is perhaps not surprising that as human beings, we do not like being told what to do. In healthcare settings traditional approaches of expert advice-giving have shown to been ineffective, with patients resisting a confrontational approach, leaving practitioners feeling powerless and not understanding the reasons for patients' ambivalence (Östlund, Wadensten, Kristofferzon, & Häggström, 2015). Miller and Rollnick (2013) distinguished providing information from advice-giving, describing advice as a special type of information which you think and recommend that the client should do. Most of the focus here is on the MI skill of providing information, but the specific skill of advice-giving is also addressed. We also consider implications for MICBT practice.

A strategy for providing information

Rollnick, Heather and Bell (1992) included 'Providing Information' as an item in their Menu of Strategies (see Chapter 27). They noted that any information provided needed to be given sensitively and that finger-wagging or taking a moralistic tone pushed the client into a corner. Rollnick et al. (1992) proposed the following steps in offering advice.

1. *Choose the right moment and ask permission.* This suggestion included the following tips:
   (a) It is best to choose a moment when the client seems curious; even better if they actually ask for information.

(b) Offer the information in a neutral way and recognise that if the client does not want to receive the information, that this is their choice.

(c) Ask permission. For example, "I wonder if you would be interested in knowing the role of your medication in managing your diabetes".

2. *Provide information in a neutral and non-personal way.* Suggestions here include presenting the information using third-party language, talking about what happens to people in general rather than what might happen to the client; and referring to what experts think or what research says, rather than providing information from what seems to be a personal perspective.

3. *Ask the person what they think.* Give the person the opportunity to respond to the information, for example by asking the question, "I wonder, what to you make of all of this?"

Elicit-provide-elicit

In recent times, MI strategy for providing information has become increasingly sophisticated. Indeed, Miller and Rollnick (2013) devoted an entire chapter to an approach which had become known as elicit-provide-elicit, or ask-tell-ask. A brief summary of key points is offered here, with readers directed to this resource for further guidance.

In terms of good practice in offering information, Miller and Rollnick (2013) suggested that MI should be about an exchange of information, in which the following assumptions are made:

- While the therapist has some expertise, clients are experts on themselves.
- Providing information should about what clients need and want.
- Information should be matched to clients' needs and strengths.
- Clients can suggest what information can be helpful.
- Advice that promotes client autonomy is preferable.

The elicit-provide-elicit (EPE) framework offers guidance for each part of the interaction.

1. *Elicit:* Ask permission and clarify the client's needs and information gaps.
2. *Provide:* Prioritise; offer the client succinct guidance; support autonomy and do not prescribe the client's response.
3. *Elicit:* Ask the client for their interpretation of the response.

Miller and Rollnick (2013) advocated that EPE should not be seen as a linear exchange, but rather a circular process, characterised by reflective listening.

Advice-giving

Miller and Rollnick (2013) suggested that advice-giving is risky, as it potentially places the therapist in the role of expert and therefore requires extra caution. Because advice-giving specifically suggests that clients should do or change something, there is increased likelihood of resistance, meaning that the therapist should be more cautious and tentative, while still adhering to the EPE structure. Miller and Rollnick (2013) emphasised the need for autonomy-supportive language in advice-giving – for example:

> *Therapist:* Well if it would help, I could tell you a bit more about the ways that research has found to be the best ways of abstaining, but only you will know what might work best for you.

Providing information within MICBT

MI is very specific on its stance on providing information, perhaps because a key area in which it developed related to the provision of medical feedback, in which the very nature of the interaction involved providing information (e.g. health screening results and their implications; the effects of non-adherence to treatment). Providing information is not within the CBT core competencies (Roth & Pilling, 2007); so using explicit MI guidance could it potentially be beneficial in supporting clients?

Atkinson (2013) suggested the following general scenarios in which providing information night be useful:

- Information about interventions (e.g. educational, medical, psychological) which might be helpful to the client.
- Signposting support for specific issues (e.g. substance use, bereavement counselling).
- Information about social, educational, vocational and leisure opportunities which might offer positive activities or social networks.
- Examples of what has helped other people. This might include offering a model-driven formulation for shared consideration.
- Resources that may be helpful, including literature, web-based resources or services offering practical support relevant to the client's situation.

Summary

1. Motivational interviewing advocates providing information in a manner which is consistent with the spirit of MI and utilises its skills, particularly reflective listening.
2. Using the EPE approach for providing information within MICBT can help promote engagement and support client autonomy.

References

Atkinson, C. (2013). Facilitating Change 2: Motivational Interviewing using the Menu of Strategies. Bath: Sodapop. Retrieved from http://www.facilitatingchange.org.uk/

de Almeida Neto, A. C. (2017). Understanding motivational interviewing: An evolutionary perspective. *Evolutionary Psychological Science, 3,* 379–389. doi:10.1007/s40806-017-0096-6

Miller, W. R., & Rollnick, S. (2013). *Motivational interviewing, third edition: Helping people change.* New York: Guilford Press.

Östlund, A. S., Wadensten, B., Kristofferzon, M. L., & Häggström, E. (2015). Motivational interviewing: Experiences of primary care nurses trained in the method. *Nurse Education in Practice, 15*(2), 111–118. doi:10.1016/j.nepr.2014.11.005

Rollnick, S., Heather, N., & Bell, A. (1992). Negotiating behaviour change in medical settings: The development of brief motivational interviewing. *Journal of Mental Health, 1,* 25–37. doi:10.3109/09638239209034509

Roth, A. D., & Pilling, S. (2007). *The competences required to deliver effective cognitive and behavioural therapy for people with depression and with anxiety disorders.* London: Department of Health.

27

Practice frameworks and the Menu of Strategies

The most recent edition of *Motivational Interviewing* (Miller & Rollnick, 2013) placed great emphasis on the spirit, processes and skills of MI but gave little attention to frameworks to guide practice, even for the inexperienced. In its infancy during the 1980s and 1990s, MI practice was complimented by a number of models and structures. These included the Drinker's Check-up (Miller & Sovereign, 1989), FRAMES (Feedback, Responsibility, Advice, Menu of Options, Empathy, Self-efficacy) (Miller & Sanchez, 1994) and a framework for negotiating behaviour change with ambivalent clients (Rollnick, Mason, & Butler, 1999). Later, however, use of these was discouraged, for fear of the core features of MI becoming lost within manualised delivery (Rollnick, Miller, & Butler, 2008). However, Atkinson and Woods (2017) proposed that the rejection of frameworks which have guided MI in the past has not been well-evidenced, and that they may indeed have utility in orientating therapy, and appeal to practitioners. With this in mind, this chapter will consider two frameworks which might offer structure to those new to MI: a beginner's guide proposed by Rollnick, Butler, Kinnersley, Gregory and Mash (2010) and the Menu of Strategies (Rollnick, Heather, & Bell, 1992).

Competent novice framework

For practitioners new to MI, Rollnick et al. (2010) proposed a guide for the "competent novice" which comprised the following steps:

Step 1 – Practise the guiding style. This step emphasises collaboration and client autonomy as well as defining the goal as eliciting change talk. It describes how this can be achieved through open-ended questions, active listening and providing information in accordance with MI practice (see Chapter 26).

Step 2 – Adding useful strategies

Four useful toolbox strategies are described, all of which are described in more detail within this book:

- Agenda setting (see Chapter 18)
- Exploring the pros and cons of changing (see Chapter 21)
- Assessing importance and confidence (see Chapter 19)
- Elicit-provide-elicit (see Chapter 26).

Step 3 – Responding skilfully to clients' language

Rollnick et al. (2010) suggested paying careful attention to client language, particularly in relation to change talk. Choosing to elicit change talk is likely to enhance motivation for change, improving the likelihood of positive outcomes. Where motivation for change is elicited, it may be appropriate to use CBT-based techniques (see Chapter 14) or planning strategies (see Chapter 20) to begin to implement a firmer plan with the client.

Menu of Strategies

The Menu of Strategies is perhaps the most well-defined practitioner framework. It was developed following concerns that practitioners were using their sense of direction within MI (Rollnick et al., 1992). The Menu offers eight distinct strategies. More than one can be used in a single meeting depending on the time available. While the original framework was developed for substance use, the description below is for a wider range of behaviours. Further information about the Menu, within the context of asking open questions, can be found in Chapter 21. The strategies are as follows, with overlaps with practice described elsewhere in the book, as indicated:

1. *Opening strategy*: This provides an opportunity to discuss current lifestyle, stresses and issues relating to the presenting concern. This activity could form part of the engaging process (see Chapter 17).

2. *Opening strategy – behaviour and context*: This is a narrower discussion about the problem behaviour and its impact. For example, a discussion about smoking could bring in wider health issues; while for a school student at risk of exclusion, it could be about their educational aspirations more generally. This strategy could link to focussing (see Chapter 18).

3. *A typical day/session*: This involves taking through the client through a typical day or behavioural episode. Atkinson (2013) proposed that exploring days and periods where the behaviour was more or less prevalent offered useful information about the context for the behaviour.

4. *The good things and the less good things*: Rollnick et al. (1992) proposed that asking about pros and cons of a behaviour in a non-judgemental way helped develop rapport and provided useful information (see Chapter 21 for question examples). They stressed the need to use neutral language, rather than refer to a problem or concern.

5. *Providing information*: The strategy is now better defined by elicit-provide-elicit (see Chapter 26).

6. *The future and the present*: This strategy asks the client to describe their preferred future (e.g. in five years' time) and then allows them to compare the current situation with these aspirations. It aims to develop discrepancy (see Chapter 9).

7. *Exploring concerns*: The most important strategy of all (Rollnick et al., 1992) relates to eliciting change talk by asking open-ended questions about concerns the client might have (see Chapter 21). Effective summarising is then used to feed this information back to the client (see Chapter 24).

8. *Helping with decision-making*: These guidelines for supporting decision-making and planning are described in full in Chapter 16, in the context of the righting reflex.

Summary

1. Protocols to support MI and CBT practice may be potentially used alongside the spirit, processes and skills to orientate the process for both therapist and client.
2. For those new to MI, protocols might be a useful way to structure their practice.
3. The framework for the Competent Novice and the Menu of Strategies are two potential frameworks which could potentially support MICBT practice.

References

Atkinson, C. (2013). Facilitating Change 2: Motivational Interviewing using the Menu of Strategies. Bath: Sodapop. Retrieved from http://www.facilitatingchange.org.uk/

Atkinson, C., & Woods, K. (2017). Establishing theoretical stability and treatment integrity for motivational interviewing. *Behavioural and Cognitive Psychotherapy*, *45*(4), 337–350. doi:10.1017/S1352465817000145

Miller, W. R. & Sovereign, R. G. (1989). Check-up: A model for early intervention in addictive behaviours. In P. T. Loberg, W. R. Miller, P. E. Nathan, & G. A. Martlett (Eds.), *Addictive Behaviour: Prevention and Early Intervention* (pp. 219–231). Amsterdam: Swets and Zeitlinger.

Miller, W. R., & Rollnick, S. (2013). *Motivational interviewing, third edition: Helping people change*. New York: Guilford Press.

Miller, W. R., & Sanchez, V. C. (1994). Motivational young adults for treatment and lifestyle change. In G. S. Howard & P. E. Nathan (Eds.), *Alcohol misuse by young adults* (pp. 51–81). Notre Dame, IN: Notre Dame Press.

Rollnick, S., Butler, C. C., Kinnersley, P., Gregory, J., & Mash, B. (2010). Motivational interviewing. *BMJ*, *340*, 1242–1245. doi:10.1136/bmj.c1900

Rollnick, S., Heather, N., & Bell, A. (1992). Negotiating behaviour change in medical settings: The development of brief motivational interviewing. *Journal of Mental Health*, *1*, 25–37. doi:10.3109/09638239209034509

Rollnick, S., Mason, P., & Butler, C. (1999). *Health behavior change: A guide for practitioners*. Edinburgh: Churchill Livingstone.

Rollnick, S., Miller, W. R., & Butler, C. C. (2008). *Motivational interviewing in health care: Helping patients change behavior*. New York: Guilford Press.

28

Training and fidelity in MICBT

There are many components to MI and CBT, so how do we know we are using them effectively and how can we develop proficiency? This chapter looks at some of the protocols and frameworks which potentially support practitioner training and development. The chapter will first consider elements of training and look at ways in which CBT practitioners can increasingly incorporate aspects of MI into their practice. It will then move on to consider how protocols for intervention fidelity can be useful in enabling skill development, facilitating reflection and offering a structure for supervision.

Training in MICBT

Csillik (2013) noted that MI was developed as communication style rather than as a set of techniques. This may make skill acquisition harder, Miller and Rollnick (2009) noting that it involves a complex skill set, which cannot be mastered through training alone. In CBT while workshops alone tend to be ineffective, more extensive training has been associated with positive changes in clinical skill (Westbrook, Sedgwick-Taylor, Bennett-Levy, Butler, & Mcmanus, 2008). In MI, the process may be lengthier, with Hall, Staiger, Simpson, Best and Lubman (2016) finding that few clinicians who had undertaken training were proficient in demonstrating the MI spirit.

Miller and Moyers (2006) identified eight sequential stages of learning MI which might be useful to CBT practitioners looking for a starting point for developing their MI practice. These are as follows:

1. The spirit of MI (see Chapter 8)
2. OARS client-centred counselling skills (see Chapters 21–24)
3. Recognising and reinforcing change talk (see Chapter 19)
4. Eliciting and strengthening change talk (see Chapter 19)
5. Rolling with resistance (see Chapter 9 for further description)
6. Developing a change plan (see Chapter 20)
7. Consolidating client commitment (see Chapters 19 and 24)
8. Switching between MI and other counselling methods (see Chapters 14 and 15).

It should be noted that while this hierarchy potentially offers a useful progression, it predates the addition of the MI processes (Chapters 17–20) into the core structure. Hall et al. (2016) suggested competency benchmarking as a way of improving proficiency in MICBT. This may be one way of ascertaining skill development and will be considered further in the next section.

Fidelity and integrity in MICBT

When looking at the effectiveness of therapy, it is impossible to know if the approach itself has impact unless it can be established that it is being used in the way described (Haddock et al., 2012). In the case of MI, this may be even more difficult. Because much of MI is based on a philosophy (the spirit) and communication (OARS) it may be possible for, for example, a manualised intervention to be delivered in accordance with guidelines, but not necessarily reflect the underlying premises of the approach (Atkinson & Woods, 2018).

Both MI and CBT have their own protocols for competency assessment. The two best known are probably the Revised Cognitive Training Scales (CTS-R) (James, Blackburn, & Reichelt, 2001) and the Motivational Interviewing Treatment Integrity (MITI) scale (Moyers, Manuel, & Ernst, 2014). The CTS-R assesses competency on both CBT-specific items (e.g. eliciting key cognitions; guided discovery), but also on 'general items', such as collaboration, and feedback. The CTS-R domain of 'interpersonal effectiveness' is based on Rogerian principles of empathy, genuineness and warmth (see Chapter 5). Links here with the person-centred principles underpinning MI are therefore clearly evident, although interpersonal effectiveness is emphasised less in CBT training and is less well-defined in the CTS-R.

The MITI offers global scales, looking at aspects of the therapeutic relationship, including 'cultivating change talk' and 'empathy' as well as behavioural counts, such as the ratio of reflections to questions, and the percentage of complex questions. Scoring against these elements can lead to judgements about levels of proficiency. While rigorous, the MITI structure is not necessarily intuitive and learning to use it requires specific training.

Haddock et al. (2012) devised the Motivational Interviewing Cognitive Training Scales (MICTS) based on these two scales to assess fidelity in integrated practice. The final scale consisted of three main sections:

1. *Procedure*: Items looked at the therapist's adherence to carrying out practical and structural aspects of a MICBT session, such as an opening discussion, agenda setting and ending the session.
2. *Process*: These items focused more on aspects of the MICBT which would be consistent with the skills and spirit of MI.
3. *Content*: This assessed particular types of intervention or strategy used.

While detailed and systematic, the complexity of all of these instruments might limit their use more to research than practice (Barwick, Bennett, Johnson, McGowan, & Moore, 2012). The final section will discuss how adapting these can enable them to be used practically to enhance therapist development in MICBT.

Fidelity versus skills development

From the perspective of developing practice, rather than assessing proficiency (e.g. for research or training purposes), Atkinson and Woods (2018) defined protocols for assessing the spirit, processes and skills of MI, which could be used for self-evaluation, peer supervision and supervision from more experienced colleagues. Although developed for use in education, they can be adapted for use in other contexts and are freely available (see Atkinson & Woods, 2019; search via the doi).

Summary

1. Because it is a communication style, MI might be harder to learn than CBT.
2. Following the eight stages of training might be one way in which CBT practitioners can become increasingly competent in MI.
3. Protocols have been developed for assessing competence in CBT, MI and MICBT. Using the actual versions, or simplified versions can be a way of helping develop therapist skills, through practice, reflection, observation and supervision.

References

Atkinson, C., & Woods, K. (2018). Integrity in the delivery of school-based motivational interviewing: protocols for practitioners. In McNamara, E. (Ed.), *Motivational interviewing with children and young people III: Education and community settings* (pp. 76–92). Ainsdale: Positive Behaviour Management.

Atkinson, C., & Woods, K. (2019). Protocols for developing practice in school-based motivational interviewing. 10.13140/RG.2.2.22951.39843

Barwick, M. A., Bennett, L. M., Johnson, S. N., McGowan, J., & Moore, J. E. (2012). Training health and mental health professionals in motivational interviewing: A systematic review. *Children and Youth Services Review*, *34*(9), 1786–1795.

Csillik, A. S. (2013). Understanding motivational interviewing effectiveness: Contributions from Rogers' client-centered approach. *Humanistic Psychologist*, *41*(4), 350–363. doi:10.1080/08873267.2013.779906

Haddock, G., Beardmore, R., Earnshaw, P., Fitzsimmons, M., Butler, R., Eisner, E., … Fitzsimmons, M. (2012). Assessing fidelity to integrated motivational interviewing and CBT therapy for psychosis and substance use: The MI-CBT fidelity scale (MI-CTS), *21*(1), 38–48. doi:10.3109/09638237.2011.621470

Hall, K., Staiger, P. K., Simpson, A., Best, D., & Lubman, D. I. (2016). After 30 years of dissemination, have we achieved sustained practice change in motivational interviewing? *Addiction*, *111*(7), 1144–1150. doi:10.1111/add.13014

James, I. A., Blackburn, I.-M., & Reichelt, F. K. (2001). *Manual of the Revised Cognitive Therapy Scale (CTS R) V12*. Northumberland: Tyne and Wear NHS Trust.

Miller, W. R., & Moyers, T. B. (2006). Eight stages in learning motivational interviewing. *Journal of Teaching in the Addictions*, *5*(1), 3–17. doi:10.1300/J188v05n01

Miller, W. R., & Rollnick, S. (2009). Ten things that motivational interviewing is not. *Behavioural and Cognitive Psychotherapy*, *37*, 129–140. doi:10.1017/S1352465809005128

Moyers, T. B., Manuel, J. K., & Ernst, D. (2014). Motivational Interviewing Treatment Integrity Coding Manual 4.1 (MITI 4.1), (December). Retrieved from http://casaa.unm.edu/download/MITI4_1.pdf

Westbrook, D., Sedgwick-Taylor, A., Bennett-Levy, J., Butler, G., & Mcmanus, F. (2008). A pilot evaluation of a brief CBT training course : Impact on trainees' satisfaction, clinical skills and patient outcomes, *36*, 569–579. doi:10.1017/S1352465808004608

29

Systemic factors in MICBT

Both MI and CBT offer a therapeutic approach for working with individuals. Notably, however, Asay and Lambert's (1999) empirical research proposed that 40% of outcome variance was due to client and extra-therapeutic factors, compared to the 30% due to therapeutic alliance and 15% to the model of delivery, both of which have been main foci within this book. While client factors refer to the characteristics and personality of the client, extra-therapeutic factors are components of the life and environment of the client which affect the likelihood of change (Thomas, 2006). Arguably, neither CBT or MI literature pays much attention to the wider factors which influence, inhibit and support change, and yet given the figures suggested by Asay and Lambert (1999), these are surely an important part of the wider intervention.

Within an educational context, Cryer and Atkinson (2015) described how it is important for therapists to spot "levers for change" outside the therapeutic relationship, which could be instrumental in improving outcomes (p. 68). With this in mind, this chapter will introduce a framework for considering how therapists can explore and support the wider factors in a client's life which affect their motivation for and ability to change.

Prochaska, Norcross and DiClemente (1994) looked at the mechanisms behind self-change and in doing so proposed nine major processes of change which included consciousness-raising about one's self and the issue; emotional arousal – experiencing and expressing feelings about problematic behaviours; and commitment – making a decision to change. Notably, four of these processes focused on systemic factors and these are detailed in Table 29.1.

Table 29.1 Systemic change processes (from Prochaska et al., 1994)

Process	Aim
Social liberation	Finding positive environments or situations where problem behaviours are not reinforced
Countering	Substituting healthy responses/behaviour for unhealthy ones
Environmental control	Restructuring the environment to reduce the probability of a problem-causing event
Helping relationships	Enlisting the help of someone who cares

While the aforementioned consciousness-raising, emotional arousal and developing commitment might typically be addressed as part of MICBT therapy, systemic factors might need additional therapist facilitation in order to offer the client an environment which is more conducive to change. These processes will now be considered in turn, in terms of how they might be operationalised to facilitate change.

Social liberation

It might be difficult for a client to change patterns of, for example, overeating or drug use, if surrounded by others who are engaging in the same behaviour, particularly during the early stages of thinking about change. Social liberation involves the client seeking situations in which the problem behaviour is forbidden, discouraged or disapproved of. Examples might include socialising with friends who are not drug users or attending facilities, such as a gym or sports club where certain behaviours (e.g. smoking, aggression) are not accepted. The client might require practical support to access these opportunities and also social skills, such as developing assertiveness skills, to refuse social invitations which may jeopardise good intentions, in order to create an environment conducive to change.

Countering

In the case of someone whose life is very much structured around a problematic behaviour, such as drinking or drug use, stopping that behaviour could potentially lead to large voids in their daily schedule, which could easily be filled by a return to the previous behaviour if alternative strategies are not provided. For example, if the client is not in work, they may find themselves with significant time on their hands, which might be used productively on some form of structured activity, such as volunteering or training. However, support may be required to access relevant activities or networks, including transport and financial assistance, which means a more holistic and multiagency response might be needed.

Environmental control

Similar to social liberation, environmental control involves helping the client to create an environment conducive to change. In some cases, this might require support for rehousing or relocating, or taking steps towards independence from a family or relationship. For others, restructuring the environment might require more straightforward adaptations, for example not keeping cigarettes or alcohol at home, changing a mobile phone number, or reorganising classroom seating arrangements so that a student sits with different peers. Factors in the environment which could compromise outcomes need identifying and addressing systematically.

Helping relationships

Change can be either supported or compromised by those closest to the client (see also Chapter 6 on self-determination theory). Prochaska et al. (1994) noted that facilitating helping relationships is not straightforward, given that very few people are trained in even the simplest helping skills. However, at a basic level, it is logical that for an individual whose drinking has become problematic, contact with people working on maintaining sobriety (for example those attending a 12-step group) is likely to be more supportive of change than, for example, socialising with heavy-drinking work colleagues. While for similar individuals, access to community support groups such as Alcoholics Anonymous might be life-changing, it is also important to look for resourceful helping relationships amongst family members and friends.

Considering systemic factors

Arguably the planning stage of MICBT (Miller & Rollnick, 2013; Roth & Pilling, 2007) offers an opportunity for the client and counsellor to both identify systemic factors and to address these specifically, through clarifying the support and resources required in order to offer the client the best chance of making and maintaining changes.

Summary

1. Research suggests that extra-therapeutic factors are important determinants of client outcomes.
2. Arguably neither MI nor CBT pay sufficient factors outside the therapeutic relationship which potentially support or compromise change.
3. Some of the change processes proposed by Prochaska et al. (1994) which consider systemic issues are potentially useful foci for planning discussions within MICBT.
4. Systemic change issues should be highlighted and tackled within the planning stage of MICBT.

References

Asay, T. P., & Lambert, M. J. (1999). The empirical case for the common factors in therapy: Quantitative findings. In M. A. Hubble, S. D. Miller, & B. L. Duncan (Eds.), *The Heart and Soul of Change: What Works in Therapy*. Washington, D.C: American Psychological Association.

Cryer, S., & Atkinson, C. (2015). Exploring the use of motivational interviewing with a disengaged primary-aged child. *Educational Psychology in Practice*, *31*(1), 56–72. doi:10.1080/02667363.2014.988326

Miller, W. R., & Rollnick, S. (2013). *Motivational interviewing, third edition: Helping people change*. New York: Guilford Press.

Prochaska, J. O., Norcross, J. C., & DiClemente, C. C. (1994). *Changing for good: a revolutionary six-stage program for overcoming bad habits and moving your life positively forward*. New York: Quill.

Roth, A. D., & Pilling, S. (2007). *The competences required to deliver effective cognitive and behavioural therapy for people with depression and with anxiety disorders*. London: Department of Health.

Thomas, M. L. (2006). The contributing factors of change in a therapeutic process. *Contemporary Family Therapy*, *28*(2), 201–210. doi:10.1007/s10591-006-9000-4

30

Ethical practice in MICBT

In this final chapter, ethical practice will be explored, within MI. Comparable guidelines for CBT practice will be compared and contrasted and practical and tangible guidance for ethical practice in MICBT will be specified.

Ethics and motivation for change

In many adult counselling interactions, clients seek support at the point at which they perceive that their behaviour is becoming problematic. For example, an individual identifying that their alcohol use has reached the point at which it threatens their relationships and employment might self-refer to a doctor in the hope of receiving medical or therapeutic support; or might phone a helpline to ask advice about next steps. Instead, MI was born out of working with clients who had not necessarily asked for support. Miller (1994) highlighted that often clients were referred for therapy because of legal ramifications associated with problematic behaviour. When considering the application of MI within school-based work, Atkinson and Woods (2003) noted that the impetus for referrals for psychological support came rarely from the students themselves, but rather from concerned adults.

This may be less of an issue in CBT where an assumption might be that the client is likely to be the concern holder. The contracting of the therapeutic relationship within MI might place greater responsibility on the therapist to be attentive to ethical issues, particularly if the client does not perceive support to be in their best interest. This has perhaps led to significant attention to ethical issues within MI. However, the authors believe that these considerations can also have implications for effective ethical practice within CBT.

Ethical issues in MI

Miller and Rollnick (2013) described how MI was originally conceptualised to deal with situations in which the therapist was working towards change, for example, reducing drinking or substance use, but the client was ambivalent, or even 'precontemplative' (see Chapter 7). In other words, the aspirations of the therapist and client potentially differed. Miller (1994, p. 111) originally identified three possible ethical issues within MI.

1. That it alters behaviour.
2. That it does so in persons not seeking or requesting change.
3. That it may operate through processes which are not immediately apparent.

Miller (1994) posed the ethical dilemma "under what circumstances and with what means is it justifiable for a therapist to proceed toward behavior change with an unmotivated individual?" (p. 114). At the same time, he argued the assumption that it would not be possible to induce change in an unmotivated client. Miller (1994) debated that while an instance where a client was a direct risk to themselves or others might be cause for unsolicited help, in less critical circumstances, intervention, particularly at a high level, might not be appropriate.

While arguably the client group typically accessing CBT may be less ambivalent about change, reference is made to "informed consent" whereby the client should be fully informed about the therapy, the CBT should be demystified and the therapist and client should work in partnership (Sookman, 2015).

When to use and not MI

At a fundamental level, Miller and Rollnick (2013) suggested that MI should be used when it can bring benefit and do no harm, stating that where there is scientific evidence to indicate that it is ineffective, that using MI would be inappropriate. Specifically Miller and Rollnick (2013) highlighted that for clients at the 'action' stage of change according to the transtheoretical model (TTM) (see Chapter 7) that research has suggested that using MI can actually compromise progress. This suggests that using the TTM as a heuristic for assessing client readiness to change should form part of the therapeutic formulation and is central to ethical practice. The application of evidence-based practice is also a significant issue in CBT ethics (Sookman, 2015).

Ethics in MICBT

Roth and Pilling (2007, p. 12) linked ethical practice to competent practice suggesting this should include "knowledge of, and ability to operate within, professional and ethical guidelines". This appears to direct practitioners to ethical frameworks linked to their professional contexts, but stops at giving CBT-specific advice. Sookman (2015) was much more precise, offering ethical guidance in relation to a number of ethical procedures, including assessment, psychoeducation, exposure and behavioural experiments; as well as in relation to more general principles, including consent, projected risk and managing boundaries. Less attention is given to 'non-specific' factors, including the therapeutic alliance.

How MI can help develop the ethics of the therapeutic relationship

It could be argued that the spirit of MI provides a sort of ethical 'code of conduct' for MICBT. In particular, the addition of the compassion element, which refers to acting in the client's best interests (Miller & Rollnick, 2013) potentially addresses some of Miller's (1994) earlier concerns. Therefore, for proponents of CBT or MICBT, it may be useful to refer to Sookman (2015) for ethical guidance on technical components and consider aspects of the MI spirit for providing greater structure for relational skills, including assessing motivation, promoting autonomy, working in partnership and supporting self-efficacy. Promotion of these factors could also help to address the power imbalance between therapist and client.

Summary

1. Particular attention to ethics may be needed for clients who are ambivalent about change.
2. Attention to ethical principles of MI and CBT is fundamental to creating a client-centred partnership and allowing the development of client autonomy and self-efficacy.
3. The MI spirit may provide a useful ethical framework for MICBT, particularly for considering relational factors and the therapeutic alliance, which may be assumed and not directly addressed in ethical guidance.

References

Atkinson, C., & Woods, K. (2003). Motivational interviewing strategies for disaffected secondary school students: A case example. *Educational Psychology in Practice*, *19*(1), 49–64. doi:10.1080/0266 736032000061206

Miller, W. R. (1994). Motivational interviewing: III. On the ethics of motivational intervention. *Behavioural and Cognitive Psychotherapy*, *22*(2), 111–123. doi:10.1017/S1352465800011905

Miller, W. R., & Rollnick, S. (2013). *Motivational interviewing, third edition: Helping people change*. New York: Guilford Press.

Roth, A. D., & Pilling, S. (2007). *The competences required to deliver effective cognitive and behavioural therapy for people with depression and with anxiety disorders.* London: Department of Health.

Sookman, D. (2015). Ethical practice of cognitive behavior therapy. In J. Z. Sadler, K. W. M. Fulford, & C. W. van Staden (Eds.), *The Oxford Handbook of Psychiatric Ethics (Volume 2)* (pp. 1293–1305). Oxford: Oxford University Press.

Index

Note: **Bold** page numbers refer to tables and *italic* page numbers refer to figures.

For Product Safety Concerns and Information please contact our EU
representative GPSR@taylorandfrancis.com Taylor & Francis Verlag GmbH,
Kaufingerstraße 24, 80331 München, Germany

Printed and bound by CPI Group (UK) Ltd, Croydon, CR0 4YY

11/04/2025
01843989-0001